FINAL MYSTERIES UNSEALED

Opening the Door to Your Destiny

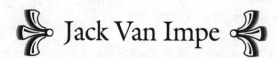

Jack Van Impe

WORD PUBLISHING

Nashville · London · Vancouver · Melbourne

Dedicated to my best friend and wife, Rexella, who, as my helpmeet, coproduced the seven-hour video on the Book of Daniel, which became the basis for this work.

Final Mysteries Unsealed

Copyright © 1998 by Jack Van Impe. All rights reserved. No portion of this book may be reproduced in any form, except for brief quotations in reviews, without written permission from the publisher.

All Scripture quotations are from the King James Version of the Bible.

Library of Congress Cataloging-in-Publication Data

Van Impe, Jack.
    Final mysteries unsealed / Jack Van Impe.
       p. cm.
    ISBN 0-8499-4043-5
    1. Bible. O.T. Daniel—Commentaries. 2. Bible O.T.
Daniel—Prophecies. I. Title.
    BS1555.3.V36 1998
    224'.5077—dc21   97-44366
                                                 CIP

Printed in the United States of America
8 9 0 1 2 3 4 5 BVG 9 8 7 6 5 4 3 2 1

FINAL MYSTERIES UNSEALED

Opening the Door to Your Destiny

Contents

Preface

I SUDDENLY AWAKENED IN the middle of the night. This sort of occurrence only happens when God places on my heart a burden to pray for someone, or when the Spirit of God enlightens my mind with a scriptural truth. On this occasion, a startling thought entered my mind—something I had neither read nor heard in all my years of research and personal Bible study.

I was astonished. *Stunned* would be a better word. At the same time, I was thrilled as God began to reveal to me: "Jack, everything Jews, Gentiles, and Christians need to know about their future is predicted in the Book of Daniel." With unusual excitement, I jumped up from my bed and spent the rest of the morning—and throughout the day—reading every verse of Daniel's great prophetic masterpiece. As I continued to read in those wee hours, I knew that God had given me a true revelation: Everything was there—all explained in the most minute detail in Daniel's twelve-chapter manuscript, penned under the anointing of the Holy Spirit.

Within a few weeks, the Spirit of God directed me to another amazing discovery through the writings of one of His prophets. This startling revelation was even greater confirmation that, because of what I was now learning, my ministry—and my life—might just never be the same. I picked up the 1935 book *Reckonings of Redemption,* by Rabbi Shvili, and read: "Everything we Jews need to know about our future is predicted in the Book of Daniel." That's the revelation God gave me in the middle of the night—in almost those exact words! I had no choice but to pursue my study of Daniel with renewed fervor and enthusiasm. After all, if these revelations were true—and I believe they are—I realized I had serious work to do.

After some three hundred hours of research—studying every book I could find, invading every conceivable theological library, and chasing down every available point of view on Daniel—most by some of the world's greatest scholars—Rexella, my wife and partner in ministry, and I organized the material on the Book of Daniel, out of which came a seven-hour video series. Because of the wide acceptance of that series, we were both pleased when Word Publishing suggested we produce a similar product in the form of a book . . . something you now hold in your hands.

Here's the very good news: The time has finally come. The Book of Daniel is now explainable and understandable. This has not always been true. In fact, as I began to study Daniel in earnest, I discovered that few scholars or commentators had ever attempted to explore this mysterious manuscript until the twentieth century. But now, finally, the hour has come to unseal the final end-time mysteries of the Book of Daniel.

None of Daniel's prophecies were to be unsealed—or understood—until the "time of the end." Imagine. Mysteries that no one could unravel for twenty-five hundred years are suddenly being presented with clarity under the anointing of the Holy Spirit. I continue to thank God for directing me to that middle-of-the-night awareness that everything Jews, Gentiles, and Christians need to know about their future is explained in the Book of Daniel. The more I read it, studied it, and prayed through it, the more I knew this was true.

Let me whet your appetite with an amazing perspective on Daniel. The first thirty-five verses of the eleventh chapter predict

135 different facts. Amazingly, each of these events has occurred and can be documented. If you check them out, you'll discover the passage to be 100 percent accurate. Even secular history documents the most minute points in this passage—right down to the names of people, places, and events.

You will also learn as you move through these pages, for example, that in Daniel 11:40–45, the king of the South (Egypt), the king of the North (Russia), and the kings of the East (the Asian confederacy) are poised to march against the leader of the West (the European Union). But when? "The time of the end," according to Daniel 11:40. Now ancient history has suddenly become modern reading. What has been sealed for twenty-five centuries is now a book with its seals removed that can be understood by any person with eyes to see and ears to hear. The message of Daniel is simply this: The clock of history is winding down. The time of the end is approaching. Daniel is a preview of coming attractions.

Major prophecies are being unsealed . . . because now is closing time. I'm glad you've joined me on what I pray will be one of the greatest, most exhilarating spiritual pilgrimages of your life as, together, we go deep into the heart and soul of Daniel and begin to tear away the veil of darkness that, for centuries, has kept these prophecies an inscrutable enigma, wrapped within an unfathomable riddle. Now God is permitting us to see them as *final mysteries unsealed.*

❧·Part I·❧

A History of the
Times . . .
And the Set-up for
Coming Attractions

❖ 1 ❖

Wanted: Healthy, Good-Looking Lads

DANIEL 1:1–3

1 *In the third year of the reign of Jehoiakim king of Judah came Nebuchadnezzar king of Babylon unto Jerusalem, and besieged it.*

2 *And the Lord gave Jehoiakim king of Judah into his hand, with part of the vessels of the house of God: which he carried into the land of Shinar to the house of his god; and he brought the vessels into the treasure house of his god.*

SWORDS FLASHED WILDLY between the nations of Egypt and Babylon, the two great military giants of the Middle East, as the latter part of the seventh century B.C. was fast coming to a close. The fierce battles between the two superpowers were visible proof that each was determined to seize full control of their part of the world. Any observer then—or historian today—knew that a decisive battle could not be far off, a conflict in which the ultimate victor would once and for all put his opponent to flight. And that's exactly what happened.

The time was early summer in the year 605 B.C. The great army of Babylon, under the leadership of Nebuchadnezzar—then crown prince—attacked the Egyptian forces in a place called Carchemish, a Babylonian city on the Euphrates River (see

Jeremiah 46 for details). It was a thorough defeat for the Egyptians, who were forced to return to their country to lick their wounds and ponder the weakness of a failed battle strategy that had brought them to their knees. With unparalleled world dominance, the Babylonians now had free reign to step into the unguarded territory of Palestine. By the summer of 605 B.C. they had wrestled control of the city of Jerusalem. And this is where our story begins.

Upon the death of Nebuchadnezzar's father, Nabopolassar, a short time after the massive Babylonian victory, Nebuchadnezzar rushed home to be crowned king of Babylon. But Nebuchadnezzar did not return to Babylon empty-handed. His saddlebags were filled with rich treasure and precious vessels—much of it taken from the holy temple in Jerusalem. His ungodly hands had pillaged the house of God, a sort of in-your-face mockery to the Holy One, a Babylonian slap in the face of the Jewish people, their traditions, and their most high God.

> *Among the choicest of Jewish young men in this group now being transported to Babylon was a teenager whose name was Daniel.*

An Opportunity for Compromise

But the man who would be king did not return with merely gold, silver, and temple utensils. Among his inventory of rich booty were also human treasures—young, fit sons of Israel who were taken from their beloved homeland and brought to Babylon, exposed to a foreign religion and traditions that bore no resemblance to their beliefs. But those were the rules of war: Lose the battle, do what your captor says. Among the choicest of Jewish young men in this group now being transported to Babylon was a teenager whose name was Daniel.

3 *And the king spake unto Ashpenaz the master of his eunuchs, that he should bring certain of the children of Israel, and of the king's seed, and of the princes;*

4 *Children in whom was no blemish, but well-favoured, and skilful in all wisdom, and cunning in knowledge, and understanding science, and such as had ability in them to stand in the king's palace, and whom they might teach the learning and the tongue of the Chaldeans.*

5 *And the king appointed them a daily provision of the king's meat, and of the wine which he drank: so nourishing them three years, that at the end thereof they might stand before the king.*

6 *Now among these were of the children of Judah, Daniel, Hananiah, Mishael, and Azariah:*

7 *Unto whom the prince of the eunuchs gave names: for he gave unto Daniel the name of Belteshazzar; and to Hananiah, of Shadrach; and to Mishael, of Meshach; and to Azariah, of Abed-nego.*

Wise Beyond His Years

Daniel now found himself a captive in a strange land, learning the language of the Chaldeans—the elite, privileged class of Babylon. Young Daniel had to accept the reality that he was now a member of a conquered people, forced to think no longer like a Jew, but like a Babylonian, with the clear demand that he give his full allegiance to Babylonian gods. This was Daniel's greatest challenge.

But in ways even Daniel could not have understood, he was more than adequately prepared for his new life. Of royal descent, Daniel had already been trained for palace service— even at his young age. He was not overwhelmed by the pomp and circumstance, nor by the tough courses he and his friends had to take in astronomy, natural history, mythology, or astrology. Gilded thrones didn't overly impress him either—he'd seen it all before.

Nebuchadnezzar simply did not know what he had on his hands: Daniel might have looked like just another strong, able Jewish boy on the outside, but the king couldn't discern who Daniel really was on the inside—a man of God, loyal and faithful to his Creator. So unswerving was Daniel's righteousness that even in the polluted atmosphere of heathen Babylon he would find a way to make himself useful to God—something we'll observe again and again as our story unfolds.

The Times of the Gentiles

Now here's a point I want to make early on because it will be critical to remember it as together we travel this amazing, prophetic road of *Final Mysteries Unsealed*. Daniel is distinctly the prophet of the "times of the Gentiles." This is significant because the "times of the Gentiles" continues on through the termination of Gentile world rule.

Daniel is not only the prophet of the Gentiles, but he's also a prophet to his own people, the Jews. When Nebuchadnezzar brought the vessels into the treasure house of his god, this was the beginning of the "times of the Gentiles," which continues until the time when Messiah returns. You may remember that Jesus said in Luke 21:24, "And they shall fall by the edge of the sword, and shall be led away captive into all nations: and

Jerusalem shall be trodden down of the Gentiles, until the *times of the Gentiles* be fulfilled" (emphasis mine). This will be a recurring theme for us throughout the book. In modern English, this is what Jesus was saying: Jerusalem will always be controlled by Gentiles—except for a brief interlude—until I return. So in 586 B.C., Nebuchadnezzar took Jerusalem, and Gentile dominion began.

From that time onward, Jerusalem would be controlled by Gentiles, with one exception—the time preceding Christ's return to set up His glorious thousand-year kingdom upon earth. This exception occurred during the miraculous victory the Jewish army experienced as they captured Jerusalem during the Six-Day War, fought June 5–10, 1967. After this military conquest, the Holy City of Jerusalem was in Jewish hands for the first time in 2,553 years.

The victory in 1967 began the countdown to Messiah's coming to rule and reign at Jerusalem (see Psalm 2:6 and Matthew 5:35). Here's why. Just before Christ appears upon the Mount of Olives to establish His glorious kingdom, all Gentile nations will gather together at the valley of Megiddo and then march to the valley of Jehoshaphat for history's final attack against Jerusalem. At this time the Gentiles temporarily retake the city. But their victory is short-lived, because then Christ appears and destroys the Gentile armies, bringing the "times of the Gentiles" to its horrendous conclusion. Christ will then reign from Jerusalem, the capital of the world, for a thousand years (see Revelation 16:16, Joel 3:2, and Zechariah 14:2–16).

Now here's the clincher. The Gentiles cannot march against Jerusalem and take it during earth's final battle if the Jews do not control the city. The Jews must be in possession of the Holy City for such an attack. This is why the Six-Day War of 1967 was so prophetically significant—it prepared the way for the battle of Armageddon and Christ's return. In a sense, I'm giving you the end of the story first, but I think it's important for you to understand this as we see the enormous impact that the Book of Daniel has on the outcome of history.

> *Young Daniel, probably no more than seventeen years old at the time of his capture, was a teenager beyond reproach.*

A Young Man of Influence

Whether the heathen king Nebuchadnezzar knew it or not, young Daniel, probably no more than seventeen years old at the time of his capture, was a teenager beyond reproach. No evil motives are ever attributed to Daniel in Scripture. Daniel had great influence on his three friends Hananiah, Mishael, and Azariah. His moral rectitude rubbed off on them, and they, too, began to demonstrate the purity that God desires for everyone, young or old. With wisdom well beyond his years, Daniel had become a mentor to his three friends. The Scripture tells us in Daniel 1:4 that Hananiah, Mishael, and Azariah were already intelligent fellows, "cunning in knowledge, and understanding science," but mere knowledge is a far cry from a mature understanding of how to apply that learning where it truly counts. But because of Daniel's daily influence, the Hebrew boys demonstrated much more than the accumulation of facts; they knew how to rely on God and to use those facts because the Spirit of almighty God was upon them. They were also fulfilling a prophecy written in Isaiah 39:7, which revealed that the offspring of the royal family of Judah would be taken as prisoners to Babylon, where they would hold high offices in the palace of the king. And this is exactly what was happening.

Can't Have Those Jewish Names, Boys

But Nebuchadnezzar had a problem. He had Jewish boys, with Jewish names, in a Babylonian palace, and he figured he'd better do something about it—especially since their very names shouted out their allegiance to their God. The name *Daniel* means "God is judge." When someone would call for Hananiah, that person would be shouting "Jehovah is gracious." Mishael's name asked the provocative question, "Who is what God is?" And Azariah's name was a constant reminder of God's mercy, meaning "Jehovah has helped."

Nebuchadnezzar couldn't allow these names to be echoed in his great hall, so he changed their names to Belteshazzar, Shadrach, Meshach, and Abed-nego. Nebuchadnezzar was the master of the quick fix. His kingly logic was, if he changed the name, he would change the person. What the king did not realize, however, was that you can change a person's name as many times as you want, but you will not necessarily change that person's heart. So the name changes were purely cosmetic, and I've got a feeling that when the boys were in their quarters, in the privacy of their conversation, they still called each other Daniel, Hananiah, Mishael, and Azariah.

In one of the great "passive resistance" protests in history, they agreed to remain unwavering in their beliefs, even if it meant taking certain life-threatening risks.

These brilliant young Jews loved their God and, as we'll look at in more detail later, boldly proclaimed His presence in their lives three times a day in prayer—with the windows wide open. They didn't care who heard them pray. They didn't care who saw them with their heads lifted to heaven. They loved their God, and they would honor Him at all costs. They remained respectful to the king, but they had a greater God to serve. In one of the great "passive resistance" protests in history, they agreed to remain unwavering in their beliefs, even if it meant taking certain life-threatening risks.

> 8 But Daniel purposed in his heart that he would not defile himself with the portion of the king's meat, nor with the wine which he drank: therefore he requested of the prince of the eunuchs that he might not defile himself.
>
> 9 Now God had brought Daniel into favour and tender love with the prince of the eunuchs.
>
> 10 And the prince of the eunuchs said unto Daniel, I fear my lord the king, who hath appointed your meat and your drink: for why should he see your faces worse liking than the children which are of your sort? then shall ye make me endanger my head to the king.
>
> 11 Then said Daniel to Melzar, whom the prince of the eunuchs had set over Daniel, Hananiah, Mishael, and Azariah,
>
> 12 Prove thy servants, I beseech thee, ten days; and let them give us pulse to eat, and water to drink.
>
> 13 Then let our countenances be looked upon before thee, and the countenance of the children that eat of

*the portion of the king's meat: and as thou seest, deal
with thy servants.*

14 *So he consented to them in this matter, and proved
them ten days.*

15 *And at the end of ten days their countenances
appeared fairer and fatter in flesh than all the children
which did eat the portion of the king's meat.*

16 *Thus Melzar took away the portion of their meat, and
the wine that they should drink; and gave them pulse.*

An Unlikely Training Food

The first challenge was what to eat for breakfast, lunch, and
dinner. Imagine the incredible feasts available to Daniel and his
friends. Delicacies galore. Meat, fowl, wine, and fruit served in
gold and silver vessels. The king's best. Who would have
refused that kind of lifestyle? Well, for starters, four young men
with the names Belteshazzar, Shadrach, Meshach, and Abed-
nego. They determined in their hearts they would not eat the
rich, fatty, high-cholesterol foods from the king's table. But
there was another reason they refused to defile their bodies:
The king's food had already been offered to the Babylonian god
Marduk, and to eat the king's food would be to break the second commandment. They knew what Exodus 20:4–5 said:

Thou shalt not make unto thee any graven image, or any
likeness of any thing that is in heaven above, or that is in the
earth beneath, or that is in the water under the earth: Thou shalt
not bow down thyself to them, nor serve them: for I the LORD
thy God am a jealous God, visiting the iniquity of the fathers
upon the children unto the third and fourth generation of them
that hate me.

But this conviction created a problem. These four boys were in training—and Nebuchadnezzar and his trainers were in charge. They were under strict orders to follow Babylonian rules, not Jewish rules. Nothing kosher here. But—and this is why I hope young people are reading this book, because this in so many ways is a young person's book—Daniel still found favor with the prince of the eunuchs. Character is what counts. Sticking to your guns when everyone else says to do something that dishonors God is what wins the day.

Now it was Melzar, the eunuch-in-charge, who had the problem. His job and his life were on the line. He had a specific assignment—to make his charges obey the rules, follow the instructions, color between the lines, do what they were told, and eat the king's food like the other Jewish boys. What could be so bad about that! "Come on, guys, please," I can almost hear him say. "I like this job, and I really don't need to get into any trouble with the head eunuch." I'm sure that Daniel and his buddies listened to their eunuch friend with hearts of compassion for the predicament he was in, but they still remained faithful to God's agenda for their lives.

We have beef, and you
want beans?

Acting Like Gentlemen

Now here's a part I love. Rather than giving Melzar a tongue-lashing, Old Testament lecture on the evils of giving good food to bad gods like Marduk, Daniel did something much more effective: He provided an alternative. He presented the eunuch an option by suggesting, "Let's just check this other idea out, and see what happens." Daniel came up with a "ten-day plan." And what was the essence of this plan? To eat only pulse—another word for beans. Beans. Not meat, fish, exotic game from the forest, rich desserts, wine flowing by the flagons—but beans . . . and water. I can just see Melzar's face turn ghostly white as he gently touches the side of his neck, wondering how long it will remain attached to the rest of his head. "Beans! Surely you jest. We have beef, and you want beans?"

Daniel and his friends confirmed their resolve, and the diet plan was approved. While the rest of Jewish captives were being wined and dined in the palace dining hall, Daniel and his three friends ate beans—and amazingly were growing stronger and healthier in mind and body day by day. They trusted their God to make them healthy and strong. They remained obedient to God when all the odds were stacked against them. And when the ten-day experiment came to an end, we read that "their countenances appeared fairer and fatter in flesh than all the children which did eat the portion of the king's meat. Thus Melzar took away the portion of their meat, and the wine that they should drink; and gave them pulse" (vv. 15–16). And the palace scoreboard read:

Daniel—1

King—0

17 As for these four children, God gave them knowledge and skill in all learning and wisdom: and Daniel had understanding in all visions and dreams.

18 *Now at the end of the days that the king had said he should bring them in, then the prince of the eunuchs brought them in before Nebuchadnezzar.*

19 *And the king communed with them; and among them all was found none like Daniel, Hananiah, Mishael, and Azariah: therefore stood they before the king.*

20 *And in all matters of wisdom and understanding, that the king inquired of them, he found them ten times better than all the magicians and astrologers that were in all his realm.*

21 *And Daniel continued even unto the first year of king Cyrus.*

There must be something about the power of beans. But for ten days? I think that's about the only diet I haven't heard about in all the hype and hoopla of today's weight management programs. Of course, the beans and water didn't make the difference—the food was simply the vehicle of faithfulness that God used to prove that He was God, and that there was no other.

Now that the experiment was over, Daniel and his friends began to focus on more serious business—such as praying to God to help them develop their gifts of wisdom, ability to discern truth from error, and the skill to differentiate between true dreams and false dreams. This was a lot for young shoulders to bear, but God was faithful to his four righteous servants, and He gave them more wisdom and knowledge than they ever could have imagined.

The Best of the Lot

We can safely assume that Daniel and his compatriots did not dine at the king's table for the entire three years of their training.

Yet, when the king took one look at Daniel and his friends, he realized there were no others in his realm who were as healthy or insightful as these four Hebrew boys. They had proved by their faithfulness to God—while maintaining an attitude of courtesy and respect for their foreign ruler—that God had sent them to the king's palace, and that they were committed to serving their God. The king quickly picked up on this, and we read that "in all matters of wisdom and understanding, that the king inquired of them, he found them ten times better than all the magicians and astrologers that were in all his realm" (1:20).

The Message for Today

What is the special word from God for us here? I believe God would have us understand that our heavenly Father wants us to be faithful, regardless of our circumstances. What if Daniel and his friends had chosen to compromise their ideals in that foreign environment? What if they had decided it made no difference to put on rolls of fat from the king's bounty, to play around with foreign gods, to engage themselves with sensuous women, and to allow their active minds to accept the ungodly mind-set of Babylonian life? If they'd taken the easy way out, they would have been ineffective servants. Just four more captives doing their time. And the king would never have honored them by saying, "I would trade ten of my best magicians and astrologers for one of these men because they have some supernatural power." Ten times better! What a recommendation. What enviable job security. And what a God-given opportunity for Daniel and his friends to begin to influence a king and the affairs of an entire kingdom at the highest level. All this was taking place because four young, God-fearing men were filled with the Spirit of God and were determined to follow His commands.

As we move from one exciting page of the Book of Daniel to the next, we'll notice that the expression, "The spirit of the gods" will appear often. As believers, we know there is only one Spirit, the blessed Holy Spirit. And when our Savior returns—a theme we'll investigate as we go along—there will be only one power. The Nebuchadnezzars of the world will have had their day. The once powerful, high, and mighty will take a backseat to the Divine Redeemer who will come for His own. At that day there will be only one power, one driving force, and one Spirit. That's why we are reminded in Ephesians 5:18 to "be filled with the Spirit." The literal Greek reads, "Be being filled with the spirit." It's a continuous process. The kind of filling that will energize you and me, just as it provided the power for Daniel to remain faithful to God during his time of trials in a foreign land. And just as Daniel stood boldly and confidently before King Nebuchadnezzar, so we have received the mandate to demonstrate the boldness of Acts 1:8: "But ye shall receive power, after that the Holy Ghost is come upon you: and ye shall be witnesses unto me both in Jerusalem, and in all Judaea, and in Samaria, and unto the uttermost part of the earth."

> *Daniel is not just a prophet from history, and his book is not just another book.*

In Daniel's day, the wisdom of the world—which was Nebuchadnezzar's world—was put to shame by the wisdom of God manifested in the lives of four committed young men. That same wisdom must be exhibited in our day—a time in history when a movement against the one true God is picking up speed and will march us to the end of the age. Daniel is not just a prophet from history, and his book is not just another book. It is our must-read guide to show us where we are heading, and the Book of Daniel will take us to a fuller understanding of the latter days and the great mysteries unsealed, beginning with Nebuchadnezzar's amazing dream of a statue and Daniel's fearless interpretation.

A King Dreams . . . A King Is Confused

DANIEL 2:1–13

1 *And in the second year of the reign of Nebuchadnezzar, Nebuchadnezzar dreamed dreams, wherewith his spirit was troubled, and his sleep brake from him.*

2 *Then the king commanded to call the magicians, and the astrologers, and the sorcerers, and the Chaldeans, for to show the king his dreams. So they came and stood before the king.*

3 *And the king said unto them, I have dreamed a dream, and my spirit was troubled to know the dream.*

4 *Then spake the Chaldeans to the king in Syriac, O king, live for ever: tell thy servants the dream, and we will show the interpretation.*

5 *The king answered and said to the Chaldeans, The thing is gone from me: if ye will not make known unto me the dream, with the interpretation thereof, ye shall be cut in pieces, and your houses shall be made a dunghill.*

6 *But if ye show the dream, and the interpretation thereof, ye shall receive of me gifts and rewards and great honour: therefore show me the dream, and the interpretation thereof.*

7 *They answered again and said, Let the king tell his servants the dream, and we will show the interpretation of it.*

8 *The king answered and said, I know of certainty that ye would gain the time, because ye see the thing is gone from me.*

9 *But if ye will not make known unto me the dream, there is but one decree for you: for ye have prepared lying and corrupt words to speak before me, till the time be changed: therefore tell me the dream, and I shall know that ye can show me the interpretation thereof.*

10 *The Chaldeans answered before the king, and said, There is not a man upon the earth that can show the king's matter: therefore there is no king, lord, nor ruler, that asked such things at any magician, or astrologer, or Chaldean.*

11 *And it is a rare thing that the king requireth, and there is none other that can show it before the king, except the gods, whose dwelling is not with flesh.*

12 *For this cause the king was angry and very furious, and commanded to destroy all the wise men of Babylon.*

13 *And the decree went forth that the wise men should be slain; and they sought Daniel and his fellows to be slain.*

PERHAPS AT SOME TIME in your life you've had a dream that was so unnerving and perplexing that it kept you from sleeping through the rest of the night. You tried to figure out what it might mean and may have even asked others to help you with an interpretation that made sense. If this has happened to you and me, we know it's happened to people throughout history.

In the year 603 B.C., King Nebuchadnezzar had a dream so bizarre that he marshaled his wisest men to his chambers to give him a reasonable interpretation. Not only did the crafty king want an interpretation of the dream he could understand, but he went one step further: He demanded a recital of the dream itself. Unreasonable? Of course. But Nebuchadnezzar was the king, and just as the gorilla sleeps anywhere it likes in the jungle, so the king could make up his own rules—which he did with an impish look in his eye, I'm sure.

Nervous Coughs and Furtive Looks

Did the king really forget the content of his dream? I doubt it. I think this was Nebuchadnezzar's way to test the wisdom and alleged supernatural powers of his magicians, astrologers, and sorcerers. Heavy has been the head that has worn the crown throughout history, and Nebuchadnezzar's crown must have weighed a ton. Kings come and go; their enemies are forever nipping at their heels. What if Nebuchadnezzar's dream were to portend evil for his realm? Superstitious as he was, he demanded an interpretation.

But there was a risk that one of the palace sorcerers might give the king information he didn't want to hear. So what does a wizard do? Equivocate? Beat around the bush? Try to buy some time? After all, the wrong information would produce disastrous results for the wizards—like being cut to pieces and having their houses made into a dunghill. But if they could state the dream and give Nebuchadnezzar an interpretation he could live with, then all manner of blessings would fall on the necromancers. So the stage was set.

I can almost hear the nervous coughs and see the furtive looks as one magician after the other would say something like, "O King, that's a marvelous idea, our telling you your dream—not that it will be easy. Say, would you mind running that dream by your servants just one more time, and then I'm sure we'll be able to come up with just the right interpretation."

> *Finally, probably with perspiration pouring from their brows, the wizards and astrologers came flat out with the truth, saying that such an assignment was impossible.*

Paranoia Abounds

The king didn't bite. He knew he had his magicians and wise men trapped, and he accused them of stalling. Finally, probably with perspiration pouring from their brows, the wizards and astrologers came flat out with the truth, saying that such an assignment was impossible—certainly too great a job for the wisest person in the realm, and one that could only be accomplished in cooperation with the gods—whose "dwelling is not with flesh" (Daniel 2:11). An interesting comment from savants who were supposed to be able to predict the future and come up with detailed—and accurate—answers to life's most perplexing problems. Yet, when push came to shove, they figured hearkening to the gods might not be such a bad idea after all. But the king didn't buy their delay and became furious. In a fit of rage he demanded that all the wise men of Babylon be rounded up and destroyed—something we've seen again and again throughout secular and religious history. When frustration mounts in the palace, scapegoats are found, and these innocents are often summarily done away with. It happened when a paranoid King Herod, intent on finding an alleged usurper to his throne, put out a decree to kill all Jewish baby boys in the land. We saw it with Hitler who, in his cruel attempt to create his Third Reich, killed six million Jews, burned all books that threatened his reign, and more than decimated all non-Aryans under his control. We saw it again just a few years ago, in the mid-to late 1960s, when an equally paranoid Chairman Mao threw all of China into convulsions with his demented "Cultural Revolution"—a nationwide witch hunt that was only an official excuse to kill and maim millions of dissidents, destroy any semblance of ancient tradition that flew in the face of his hybrid communism, and put China on a crash course with history. Will tyrants ever learn?

Now, the net was thrown wide throughout the kingdom of Nebuchadnezzar to bring all the men of wisdom to their knees and ultimately to their collective death. Although it appears that Daniel and his friends were not in this shouting session with the king, they were, in fact, to be included in the king's order. The great irony of the king's manifesto as it related to Daniel was that once again God was setting the stage for a display of His sovereignty over the affairs of men. Meanwhile, the hunt was on.

14 *Then Daniel answered with counsel and wisdom to
  Arioch the captain of the king's guard, which was
  gone forth to slay the wise men of Babylon:*

15 *He answered and said to Arioch the king's captain,
Why is the decree so hasty from the king? Then
Arioch made the thing known to Daniel.*

16 *Then Daniel went in, and desired of the king that he
would give him time, and that he would show the
king the interpretation.*

17 *Then Daniel went to his house, and made the thing
known to Hananiah, Mishael, and Azariah, his companions:*

18 *That they would desire mercies of the God of heaven
concerning this secret; that Daniel and his fellows
should not perish with the rest of the wise men of
Babylon.*

19 *Then was the secret revealed unto Daniel in a night
vision. Then Daniel blessed the God of heaven.*

20 *Daniel answered and said, Blessed be the name of
God for ever and ever: for wisdom and might are his:*

21 *And he changeth the times and the seasons: he
removeth kings, and setteth up kings: he giveth wisdom unto the wise, and knowledge to them that know
understanding:*

22 *He revealeth the deep and secret things: he knoweth
what is in the darkness, and the light dwelleth with
him.*

23 *I thank thee, and praise thee, O thou God of my
fathers, who hast given me wisdom and might, and
hast made known unto me now what we desired of
thee: for thou hast now made known unto us the
king's matter.*

24 *Therefore Daniel went in unto Arioch, whom the king had ordained to destroy the wise men of Babylon: he went and said thus unto him; Destroy not the wise men of Babylon: bring me in before the king, and I will show unto the king the interpretation.*

> *Daniel went back to his quarters and held an impromptu prayer meeting/counseling session with his companions Hananiah, Mishael, and Azariah.*

Daniel's Strategy

We've now begun to see the sterling character of Daniel. Though still young, he was wise beyond his years; though relatively inexperienced in the affairs of life, he demonstrated how God can use a servant who gives his absolute loyalty to the Father. Now, it was again Daniel's turn to settle uncontrollable waters. Here's where we as believers need to take careful note of Daniel's spiritual strategy. First, he asked for time—always a good idea when we are trying to come up with a solution to one of life's challenges. Second, he was bold enough to say that he would fulfill the king's demand—that is, he promised to do what the other wise men could not. Daniel knew that with God on his side he was not stepping out on a partially sawed-off limb. He knew his heavenly Father would give him the insight required at the time he would need it. Third—and how often we fail to do this—Daniel went back to his quarters and held an impromptu prayer meeting/counseling session with his companions Hananiah, Mishael, and Azariah. Proverbs 15:22 reminds us, "Without counsel purposes are disappointed: but in the multitude of counsellors they are established." Daniel knew the importance of feedback from his companions—an awareness that runs throughout the entire book.

Daniel's "Model Prayer"

Now I want you to pay special attention to Daniel's prayer—just one of the many prayers of this great man of God we will discover in the pages of this amazing prophecy. Remember, Daniel already believed that God would give him the answer he'd need when he would soon stand before the king. He'd already conferred with his friends and received their counsel. But Daniel knew that unless he prayed earnestly to his God for divine insight and wisdom, he would never be prepared for his daunting assignment with a paranoid king.

For years, I've felt this prayer of Daniel should be a model for our own time with God—a prayer that moves me anew as I read it again, perhaps for the thousandth time. Daniel blesses God for His wisdom. He acknowledges that earthly kings are just that—as common as dirt—and that God alone sets up rulers and brings them crashing down from their man-made thrones. He recognizes that only His God—not Marduk, or any other Babylonian idol—gives wisdom to the wise and has the necessary resources to bring light to that which is shrouded in darkness. Then, in a final burst of praise, Daniel thanks God for the wisdom and might He's given to His servant. Daniel thanks God—giving no credit to himself—for the answers he now has to King Nebuchadnezzar's dream. Can't you just hear Daniel's prayer build with confidence as he moves toward his final crescendo—his glorious amen to his God?

> *Daniel, a young man with*
> *limited life experience, is*
> *now used by God to shape the*
> *destiny of an entire kingdom.*

Ready to Meet the King

Daniel has done his homework. He's been patient. He's prayed. Now he's ready with an exuberance and confidence that can only come to a believer in the one true God. Only after this serious, pre-audience preparation does Daniel finally say to Arioch, "All right, now's the time. I'm ready to enter the presence of the king . . . and by the way, make sure that the king spares the lives of the wise men of Babylon. There's now no reason for them to die." Daniel, a young man with limited life experience, is now used by God to shape the destiny of an entire kingdom.

The apostle Paul, hundreds of years later, would say to another young man, Timothy, "Let no man despise thy youth; but be thou an example of the believers, in word, in conversation, in charity, in spirit, in faith, in purity" (1 Timothy 4:12). In God's eyes, age has little significance when it comes to being a wise servant. Just as He did then, all God demands from His people is obedience. This spirit would be the hallmark of the man Daniel to the end of his days.

25 *Then Arioch brought in Daniel before the king in*
haste, and said thus unto him, I have found a man of
the captives of Judah, that will make known unto the
king the interpretation.

26 The king answered and said to Daniel, whose name
was Belteshazzar, Art thou able to make known unto
me the dream which I have seen, and the interpretation thereof?

27 Daniel answered in the presence of the king, and said,
The secret which the king hath demanded cannot the
wise men, the astrologers, the magicians, the soothsayers, show unto the king;

28 But there is a God in heaven that revealeth secrets,
and maketh known to the king Nebuchadnezzar what
shall be in the latter days. Thy dream, and the visions
of thy head upon thy bed, are these;

29 As for thee, O king, thy thoughts came into thy mind
upon thy bed, what should come to pass hereafter:
and he that revealeth secrets maketh known to thee
what shall come to pass.

30 But as for me, this secret is not revealed to me for any
wisdom that I have more than any living, but for their
sakes that shall make known the interpretation to the
king, and that thou mightest know the thoughts of thy
heart.

Glory to God Alone

Daniel now had the king's attention. He also continued to
remind the king that the wisdom he was sharing was from the
one true God and not from his own knowledge. What integrity!
Daniel could have made this a public relations spectacular for
himself by taking all the credit, comparing himself to the other
wise men (who failed to speak the dream or interpret it), saying,
"Hey, King, look at me. I'm the man. You can always count on
me for the answers to your tough questions."

But that is not the Daniel of this book. He took no glory for himself, but instead insisted that only God in heaven could do what the king had requested. I can almost see King Nebuchadnezzar's mouth begin to drop as Daniel set him up. Nebuchadnezzar was probably saying something like, "Come on, Daniel, enough of this 'My God' stuff. What's my dream? More importantly, what does it mean? And why are you making me wait?" But Daniel was not to be rushed. He was in control of this particular discussion and, once again, the king was compelled to wait for the time when this young Jew would come forth with his secrets, which he finally shared when he said:

31 *Thou, O king, sawest, and behold a great image. This great image, whose brightness was excellent, stood before thee; and the form thereof was terrible.*

32 *This image's head was of fine gold, his breast and his arms of silver, his belly and his thighs of brass,*

33 *His legs of iron, his feet part of iron and part of clay.*

34 *Thou sawest till that a stone was cut out without hands, which smote the image upon his feet that were of iron and clay, and brake them to pieces.*

35 *Then was the iron, the clay, the brass, the silver, and the gold, broken to pieces together, and became like the chaff of the summer threshingfloors; and the wind carried them away, that no place was found for them: and the stone that smote the image became a great mountain, and filled the whole earth.*

I imagine the king was startled, and dumbfounded, probably exclaiming something like, "I can't believe this, Daniel. You're a genius! You've done what my most seasoned astrologers and magicians could not do. You're amazing . . . and you're still so young!"

But there is a God in heaven that revealeth secrets.

Daniel just stood there and listened politely, continuing to assert that God gave him the dream. He probably reminded the king of what he'd already told him, "But there is a God in heaven that revealeth secrets"(2:28). Wouldn't you like to have seen Nebuchadnezzar's face as Daniel spoke the dream one scene at a time? The king's heart rate must have increased as Daniel talked about an image so large and brilliant that it was virtually impossible to look at for any length of time. His blood pressure must have climbed as Daniel described the statue from head to foot—the head of gold; breast and arms of silver; belly and thighs of brass; legs of iron; and feet and toes of an unstable mixture of iron and clay.

The Dream Interpreted

Then, thundering from a distance came a stone cut out without hands—that is, not of human origin—crashing into the statue with such meteoric force that it dissolved the image into chaff, blowing away any semblance of the statue. Where the image had stood—this is what had to give King Nebuchadnezzar pause—the stone, now a large mountain, "filled the whole earth" (2:35). If you were a superstitious Babylonian king constantly looking over your shoulder at the slightest movement of your enemies—or wondering if inside-the-palace intrigue might one day do you in—what would you think if you had a dream like this? Without waiting for the king's response—or perhaps because Nebuchadnezzar was too dumbfounded to respond—Daniel proceeded with the interpretation of his dream.

36 *This is the dream; and we will tell the interpretation thereof before the king.*

37 *Thou, O king, art a king of kings: for the God of heaven hath given thee a kingdom, power, and strength, and glory.*

38 *And wheresoever the children of men dwell, the beasts of the field and the fowls of the heaven hath he given into thine hand, and hath made thee ruler over them all. Thou art this head of gold.*

39 *And after thee shall arise another kingdom inferior to thee, and another third kingdom of brass, which shall bear rule over all the earth.*

40 *And the fourth kingdom shall be strong as iron: forasmuch as iron breaketh in pieces and subdueth all things: and as iron that breaketh all these, shall it break in pieces and bruise.*

41 *And whereas thou sawest the feet and toes, part of potters' clay, and part of iron, the kingdom shall be divided; but there shall be in it of the strength of the iron, forasmuch as thou sawest the iron mixed with miry clay.*

42 *And as the toes of the feet were part of iron, and part of clay, so the kingdom shall be partly strong, and partly broken.*

43 *And whereas thou sawest iron mixed with miry clay,*
they shall mingle themselves with the seed of men: but
they shall not cleave one to another, even as iron is
not mixed with clay.

44 *And in the days of these kings shall the God of heaven*
set up a kingdom, which shall never be destroyed: and
the kingdom shall not be left to other people, but it
shall break in pieces and consume all these kingdoms,
and it shall stand for ever.

45 *Forasmuch as thou sawest that the stone was cut out*
of the mountain without hands, and that it brake in
pieces the iron, the brass, the clay, the silver, and the
gold; the great God hath made known to the king
what shall come to pass hereafter: and the dream is
certain, and the interpretation thereof sure.

Not So Fast, O King

Daniel was anything but timid, for God had removed any spirit of fear from his heart as he stood eye-to-eye with Nebuchadnezzar, giving him the message from God. Nebuchadnezzar undoubtedly saw himself as a self-made king—powerful, in control, able to make heads roll at a snap of his finger. Yet Daniel says, "Wait a minute, King. Not so fast. You are only where you are because my God has given you dominion, power, and glory. Yes, you're a mighty and powerful king, but your reign simply cannot last." Daniel consistently gives God the credit in the preface of all his prayers and speeches. The king would probably rather not have to sit there and listen to these extended preambles, but this was young Daniel's moment. And Nebuchadnezzar would have to be patient.

Daniel's description of Babylon's place in world history is fully in sync with other historical references. Babylon was the greatest power of the day. It had always been a superlative empire, with its great beauty, economic position as a center of commerce, and fabled hanging gardens—one of the exquisite wonders of the ancient world. But even all these accomplishments, Daniel would argue, were not Nebuchadnezzar's doing—but God's. Although Nebuchadnezzar was the "gold head" in his dream, the inference was that he would not be in charge of his kingdom in perpetuity: Daniel's message was that God was in control, and that his heavenly Father would have the final say as to who would and who would not occupy all earthly thrones—including Nebuchadnezzar's.

> *We should not be surprised to note that Daniel's prophecy became reality when Medo-Persia brought Babylon to its knees in military defeat in 539 B.C.*

Kingdoms Come . . . Kingdoms Go

Marduk, Babylon's chief god, was also called the "god of gold"—something that surely did not escape the king's notice. In fact, the precious metal gold was almost synonymous with the nation of Babylon. There was gold everywhere—in the ornate palaces, the worship places, and the ubiquitous shrines. Even the walls were overlaid with what was then the most precious substance in existence. Now King Nebuchadnezzar was told that all this gold would one day be swept away by a second kingdom, the kingdom of Medo-Persia.

This later became a historic fact when the two disparate cultures—the Medes and the Persians—united in 550 B.C. under one king to form a great world power. This was the "silver" part of the statue and a proper representation of the Medo-Persian empire since the Medes and Persians based their partnership on the power of money collected through an elaborate system of taxation. Nebuchadnezzar must have been relieved to hear Daniel prophesy that this "silver" kingdom would be inferior to his own, probably because as a partnership nation, Medo-Persia did not have the political and military unity of Babylon. But despite this weakness, Medo-Persia would one day break the "head of gold." Because God's Word speaks only the truth, we should not be surprised to note that Daniel's prophecy became reality when Medo-Persia brought Babylon to its knees in military defeat in 539 B.C.

But what about the third kingdom, the belly and thighs of brass? The element bronze later became a characterization of the Greek empire, primarily because the Greeks used it extensively as the material for their weapons of war. Daniel foresaw that Greece would one day "bear rule over all the earth" (2:39). History shows that Greece did dominate the world of its day. Alexander the Great's kingdom encompassed much more of the known world than Babylon or Medo-Persia ever did. Again, a prophecy of Daniel was fulfilled in world history.

The Renewal of the Roman Empire

Imagine how Nebuchadnezzar must have reacted to the news from this young prophet. His was probably a mixture of fear and disbelief. But we must also note that Daniel wasn't finished yet, and the king did not interrupt Daniel's interpretation.

After the world-dominating empire of bronze another empire would arise—a fourth kingdom composed of two legs of iron. This kingdom would be Rome with its "two legs" representing the expansive empires of the Western Roman Empire, headquartered in Rome, and the Eastern Roman Empire, with the cosmopolitan city of Constantinople as its capital. This empire also would fall. The great historian Edward Gibbon powerfully describes it in his work entitled *The Decline and Fall of the Roman Empire*. However, just before Christ returns, this empire will revive as the iron mixed with clay begins to wiggle in the form of ten toes.

Only God could have given Daniel the wisdom to know what is now becoming reality for us who live in the latter days of the twentieth century. According to Daniel, the final revival of the Roman Empire would be comprised of a confederation of ten nations, which would finally lead to a new world order encompassing the globe. Why would they come together? For monetary and military security and strength—something we're already seeing as the European Union moves ahead with such plans at break-neck speed. Thus, Nebuchadnezzar's image with ten toes pictured the revival and conclusion of the Roman Empire.

The world in which you and I live—the world of the fourth and revived fifth kingdom as prophesied by Daniel—is going to get worse up to the moment that the great stone breaks the feet of the image.

Note the gradual deterioration of the metals in Nebuchadnezzar's dream: from gold to silver to bronze to iron to clay, a clear demonstration that as history marches on, men and their cultures become increasingly corrupt. Tregelles is a scholar who has called attention to the decreasing "specific gravity" of each of these metals: For example, the specific gravity of gold is 19; silver, 11; brass, 8.5; cast iron, 7.8; mixture of iron and clay, 1.93. The world in which you and I live—the world of the fourth and revived fifth kingdom as prophesied by Daniel—is going to get worse up to the moment that the great stone breaks the feet of the image. That stone is Jesus Christ, who becomes a mountain and fills the entire earth. "And in the days of these kings shall the God of heaven set up a kingdom, which shall never be destroyed: and the kingdom shall not be left to other people, but it shall break in pieces and consume all these kingdoms, and it shall stand for ever" (2:44).

The Ten Toes Begin to Wiggle

The entire end-time message is predicted here in the Book of Daniel thousands of years, in some instances, before the actual historical events occurred—just as Rabbi Shvili in 1935 suggested in his book, *Reckonings of Redemption*. How could Daniel know this? Because God, historically, has chosen to reveal His secrets through spirit-anointed prophets.

Let's bring Daniel's prophecy even closer to home. There was a long interval between the time when Rome's power began to wane and fall—around 476 A.D.—and the year 1947 when the "ten toes" of the statue began to wiggle. First of all, Benelux met in that year—Belgium, the Netherlands, and Luxembourg—creating the first three members of the confederation. In 1957, three additional nations met with the countries of Benelux—Italy, France, and Germany—for a total of six, ratified by the Treaty of Rome. Little by little, in our daily newspapers, we see a revival of the Roman Empire just as Daniel predicted. In 1973, England, Ireland, and Denmark joined the confederation, making it a total of nine members. Then, on New Year's Day, 1981, Greece became number ten. The time that Daniel prophesied is here. We are living in the latter days, and Jesus is coming soon.

Jesus Is Our Rock

One of the most profound messages of these verses is that you and I don't have to worry about straightening out our world. We have almighty God, Adonai, who is in charge of the affairs of earth. Jesus is the rock, that stone, on which the true church is built. You'll remember in Matthew that Jesus asked the apostle Peter, "Whom do men say that I am?" Peter answered, "You are the Christ, the Son of God." And Jesus said, "On this rock I will build my church" (see 16:13–18). Christ was that rock (1 Corinthians 10:4). Yes, the rock in Nebuchadnezzar's dream that eventually engulfs the entire world, a rock that will hit the feet, not the head—Babylon; not the chest and arms of silver—the Medes and the Persians; not the stomach and thighs of brass—Greece; not the legs of iron—Rome. They went out of existence. Instead, the rock strikes that group that revives at the time of the end—the ten toes, the restored Roman Empire. Thus, on January 1, 1981, when Greece became number ten, pictured by the ten toes on the image, we were given the clearest signal yet that we were headed toward the end times and would soon be ushered into an environment that would be ready for the return of Christ as King of Kings and Lord of Lords (Revelation 19:16).

One of the reasons the Book of Daniel is so important is that it provides us with a complete scenario for the end times.

God's Sovereignty

We can therefore reasonably conclude that the dream of Daniel chapter two reveals that the Kingdom of God will soon be established in connection with the second coming of our Savior. Daniel 2:44 states, and I repeat this for the sake of emphasis, "And in the days of these kings shall the God of heaven set up a kingdom, which shall never be destroyed: and the kingdom shall not be left to other people, but it shall break in pieces and consume all these kingdoms, and it shall stand for ever." It's all starting to happen. Just as the image in Nebuchadnezzar's dream contained metals that degraded as they descended from gold to iron and clay, so will the world in which you and I live become increasingly apostate and the more our society at large will be governed by outright militarism as its only vehicle to control the violence that is present and that is yet to come.

What was the actual purpose of Nebuchadnezzar's dream? To show God's sovereign rule over the affairs of men, leading to the future Gentile world domination and its ultimate destruction, to be replaced by a Kingdom and a King who would reign forever on earth (Matthew 6:10).

One of the reasons the Book of Daniel is so important is that it provides us with a complete scenario for the end times. And it all begins to wind down with the current revival of the Roman Empire, which I believe is the present-day European Union. After this episode is completed, there is no more. This will be the last empire, and it will continue into the latter days, with the Antichrist as the primary figure taking over the resurrected Roman Empire (Revelation 17:10). He will be a dictator of world proportions and will rule the world of his day just as King Nebuchadnezzar ruled his world as leader of Babylon. But for those of us who know the whole story, we need not fear the perilous times yet to come because "the stone [which] was cut out of the mountain without hands" (2:45) is none other than the person of Jesus Christ, God's anointed, our Savior, the Rock of our salvation. When He returns to gather His own, God will establish His Kingdom which will prevail in our world, and for a thousand years all beings on earth will be tremendously blessed under the personal reign of the Lord Jesus Christ.

46 Then the king Nebuchadnezzar fell upon his face, and worshipped Daniel, and commanded that they should offer an oblation and sweet odours unto him.

47 The king answered unto Daniel, and said, Of a truth it is, that your God is a God of gods, and a Lord of kings, and a revealer of secrets, seeing thou couldest reveal this secret.

48 Then the king made Daniel a great man, and gave him many great gifts, and made him ruler over the whole province of Babylon, and chief of the governors over all the wise men of Babylon.

49 Then Daniel requested of the king, and he set Shadrach, Meshach, and Abed-nego, over the affairs of the province of Babylon: but Daniel sat in the gate of the king.

Daniel's God Is Greatest!

Nebuchadnezzar's subjects often fell on their faces before their leader, but for the king to subject himself to such a humble posture meant that Daniel had indeed gotten through to him. It also appeared that Nebuchadnezzar may have been making some spiritual progress, revealed by his act of contrition, admitting that Daniel's God was the greatest god of all. The king made good on his promise that he would reward the wise one who met the demands of speaking and interpreting his dream, and Daniel was subsequently exalted throughout the realm. But Daniel, always a man of integrity, did not forget his friends, and requested that the king give them key positions as well. His wish was granted. Daniel continued to be a person of great influence in the king's court by being allowed to sit in the gate of the king—a position of judge, the equivalent of a Supreme Court justice and confidant of the king. Yet Daniel never compromised his standards in that foreign land.

Through it all, Daniel remained faithful to his God, continuing to speak the truth fearlessly, always serving notice to Nebuchadnezzar that God alone, not earthly kings, has the real power. God does not tremble at the sight of monarchs. If anything, He laughs at their rebellion, and in Psalm 2:1–4—a passage that pictures the battle of Armageddon—we read: "Why do the heathen rage, and the people imagine a vain thing? The kings of the earth set themselves, and the rulers take counsel together, against the LORD, and against his anointed, saying, Let us break their bands asunder, and cast away their cords from us. He that sitteth in the heavens shall laugh: the LORD shall have them in derision."

But kings will be kings. Seemingly a victim of short-term memory, Nebuchadnezzar goes on yet another rampage. During his recurring paranoia he commands that his servants turn up the heat in the palace furnace seven times hotter. It's a futile attempt to destroy three Hebrew teenagers—surely one of the most fascinating and familiar stories in all the Bible, and a dramatic preview of the real wrath that is yet to come during the Tribulation hour—another mystery which we will see unsealed.

·3·

Unfazed by the Furnace

DANIEL 3:1–7

1 Nebuchadnezzar the king made an image of gold,
   whose height was threescore cubits, and the breadth
   thereof six cubits: he set it up in the plain of Dura, in
   the province of Babylon.

2 Then Nebuchadnezzar the king sent to gather together
   the princes, the governors, and the captains, the
   judges, the treasurers, the counsellors, the sheriffs, and
   all the rulers of the provinces, to come to the dedication of the image which Nebuchadnezzar the king had
   set up.

3 Then the princes, the governors, and captains, the
   judges, the treasurers, the counsellors, the sheriffs, and
   all the rulers of the provinces, were gathered together
   unto the dedication of the image that Nebuchadnezzar
   the king had set up; and they stood before the image
   that Nebuchadnezzar had set up.

4 Then an herald cried aloud, To you it is commanded,
   O people, nations, and languages,

5 That at what time ye hear the sound of the cornet,
   flute, harp, sackbut, psaltery, dulcimer, and all kinds

> *of music, ye fall down and worship the golden image*
> *that Nebuchadnezzar the king hath set up:*
>
> 6 *And whoso falleth not down and worshippeth shall*
> *the same hour be cast into the midst of a burning fiery*
> *furnace.*
>
> 7 *Therefore at that time, when all the people heard the*
> *sound of the cornet, flute, harp, sackbut, psaltery, and*
> *all kinds of music, all the people, the nations, and the*
> *languages, fell down and worshipped the golden*
> *image that Nebuchadnezzar the king had set up.*

WE SAID EARLIER that kings will be kings, and Nebuchadnezzar was no exception. One moment Daniel had Nebuchadnezzar's undivided attention, almost persuading him of the ultimate power of the one, true God; the next minute, the king was again egocentric and self-promoting, forgetting Daniel's prophecy and its implications. Perhaps the king was simply denying his mighty Babylonian kingdom would ever really collapse—especially at the hands of the Medo-Persian empire.

A Preview of 666

Imagine the sight of a golden image of Nebuchadnezzar that was ninety feet high (sixty cubits) and nine feet wide (six cubits in all, a cubit being approximately eighteen inches), erected on the plain of Dura. While the golden image may simply have appeared to be little more than a massive statue, it actually holds great prophetic meaning and is yet another end-time mystery about to be unsealed. For example, the numbers 66 come together here: the number of man (sixty cubits high) and six cubits wide, resembling the number of the Antichrist in Revelation 13:16–18 (six cubits). This gives us a reference to the time when the Antichrist comes into power and his false prophet sets up an image of his likeness in the temple. Revelation 13:15 says, "And he had power to give life unto the image of the beast, that the image of the beast should both speak, and cause that as many as would not worship the image of the beast should be killed."

Faucet's Bible Dictionary Encyclopedia reports that the archaeologist Opert once journeyed to present day Iraq—the area of biblical Babylon—and excavated what most evangelical scholars believe is the pedestal on which Nebuchadnezzar's great image had been placed—proving this biblical event really happened! Some believe the gold statue may have been built to honor Nebuchadnezzar's deceased father, Nabopolassar. Others suggest it was erected to appease Bel or Marduk—the revered pagan gods of Babylon. More likely, the image was a representation of the king himself. Nebuchadnezzar had a flair for publicity, and he knew where to position the gigantic statue so that no one could miss seeing it. While Babylon was a sky-scraper city of its day, the plain of Dura was a huge mound of earth, about six miles southeast of Babylon, probably a walled area that Nebuchadnezzar could have easily used as a focal point to stage an event of this enormity. Anything constructed in that area would be seen for miles around. Its strategic position allowed for thousands of people to descend on the area at once, thus giving the king a venue for a mass rally where loyal supporters could bow and pay their homage to the king. This seemed to be a carefully planned "photo op" for Nebuchadnezzar, and an event which all the chief officers of the land were commanded to attend—including Daniel's three friends, Shadrach, Meshach, and Abed-nego.

> *During the tribulation hour, the Antichrist will make an image of himself (Revelation 13:15), and anyone who will not worship that image will be killed.*

Fail to Bow . . . Pay the Price

Here we catch a glimpse of Nebuchadnezzar's political acumen and get a dramatic preview of the activities of the Antichrist to come. The king knew he had to keep certain conquered peoples under his thumb at all times, and what better vehicle than native religion to promote the power of the state? Nebuchadnezzar knew that whatever officials saw that day on the plain of Dura, they would take back to those captives under their jurisdiction. Apparently Daniel was somewhere else in the realm on business for the king, since he was not present at the unveiling of the golden image. In fact, Daniel is not even mentioned in this chapter. For the first time in our story, his three friends are on their own. But because Daniel had exerted such great moral and spiritual influence on his companions, compromise with foreign gods was out of the question.

However, these three faithful Hebrews would pay a terrible price for not bowing to the image. King Nebuchadnezzar would try to have them killed, picturing an approaching day when the Antichrist carries out the same penalty on those who refuse to bow to his image and reject his mark, 666. At first reading this passage simply appears to be a provocative piece of biblical history. Closer observation, however, tells us that this story speaks to where you and I are today—and where we are quickly headed.

For instance, during the Tribulation hour, the Antichrist will make an image of himself (Revelation 13:15), and anyone who will not worship that image will be killed, even as those who refused to bow to the image of Nebuchadnezzar were threatened with destruction in a furnace of fire. The only difference between the two events is magnitude. The Tribulation hour will be a time when fire engulfs the earth. Revelation 8:7 says, "And the third part of trees was burnt up, and all green grass was burnt up." Revelation 9:18 tells us, "By these three was the third part of men killed, by the fire, and by the smoke, and by the brimstone." Accompanying all this mayhem will be the Antichrist, who says, "If you don't worship me and my image, you're going to die." Revelation 20:4 says, "And I saw thrones, and they sat upon them, and judgment was given unto them: and I saw the souls of them that were beheaded for the witness of Jesus, and for the word of God, and which had not worshipped the beast, neither his image."

Matthew 25:31–46, however, declares that there will be multitudes who will survive the seven-year period without taking the number. I'm not sure how, but they will persevere, just as the three Hebrew children ultimately survived their trial by fire.

Nebuchadnezzar—Picture of the Antichrist

So the statue on the plain of Dura was more than just an image of a king. It graphically represented the king's continued rebellion against God—just as the Antichrist will become the definition of rebellion against the Almighty. The image also indicated that the king was egocentric, offering his image to the people as a symbol of self-deification. Again, there are Antichrist implications (Daniel 11:36). Politically, Nebuchadnezzar needed a strong, unifying force to continue to bring together the disparate tribes and nations that fell to the power of Babylon. In short, Nebuchadnezzar's purpose was to institute a totalitarian regime, and this was one way to galvanize the people's attention and allegiance. What better description can we find in Scripture of the political prowess of the Antichrist to come!

To remain standing in
defiance of the king's order
would mean certain death
in a fiery furnace.

Not surprisingly, when the word went out that this was "bow down" time, the officials, governors, and whoever else had managed to get to Dura that day paid obeisance to the king right on cue. Imagine the scene. Nebuchadnezzar was so fully in control of this grand event that he even had it choreographed. When the conductor of this desert orchestra of cornets, flutes, harps, sackbuts (stringed instruments), psalteries, and dulcimers lowered his baton, it was time to fall to one's knees. And that's what the masses did: They looked at the great statue, and they fell down to worship. Why not? To remain standing in defiance of the king's order would mean certain death in a fiery furnace.

Three Young Men Who Refused to Compromise

No exceptions to the king's rule would be tolerated. Now, once again, Daniel's three friends had to make a decision. They knew the Scriptures, and I'm sure their minds were racing to the first two commandments of Moses they'd memorized years before from the Book of Exodus: "Thou shalt have no other gods before me. Thou shalt not make unto thee any graven image, or any likeness of any thing that is in heaven above, or that is in the earth beneath, or that is in the water under the earth" (Exodus 20:3–4).

For these three Hebrew children that was all they needed to remember. It was no longer a dilemma. They had always obeyed the law of God. Daniel served under six kings and always honored them—even when their point of view differed with some of his own opinions. But on the question of allegiance to the God of Israel, Daniel never compromised. Early on, his three Hebrew friends had also refused to compromise. Rather than worry about incurring the wrath of an earthly king, their greater concern was that they not subject themselves to the wrath of their living God. Now, once again, even as they had earlier refused to eat the rich food from the king's table, Shadrach, Meshach, and Abed-nego refused to sacrifice their respect for God's law on a pagan altar.

8 *Wherefore at that time certain Chaldeans came near, and accused the Jews.*

9 *They spake and said to the king Nebuchadnezzar, O king, live for ever.*

10 *Thou, O king, hast made a decree, that every man that shall hear the sound of the cornet, flute, harp, sackbut, psaltery, and dulcimer, and all kinds of music, shall fall down and worship the golden image:*

11 *And whoso falleth not down and worshippeth, that he should be cast into the midst of a burning fiery furnace.*

12 *There are certain Jews whom thou hast set over the affairs of the province of Babylon, Shadrach, Meshach, and Abed-nego; these men, O king, have not regarded thee: they serve not thy gods, nor worship the golden image which thou hast set up.*

*Get the furnace ready for
three young Hebrews.*

The people who bowed to the ruling powers had a problem with our three Hebrew friends Shadrach, Meshach, and Abednego. Jealousy and a large dose of anti-Semitism were factors in their dislike of these foreigners who had been given lofty positions by the king. Undoubtedly, some of these threatened Chaldeans snitched on Daniel's companions, and before long, word of the Hebrews' insubordination was passed on to the king. Their charge: rebellion against the king and the law of the land. And what better proof of the allegation than the fact that the young men had remained standing before the image while Nebuchadnezzar's minions lay flat on their faces in worship. Get the furnace ready for three young Hebrews.

13 *Then Nebuchadnezzar in his rage and fury commanded them to bring Shadrach, Meshach, and Abed-nego.
Then they brought these men before the king.*

14 *Nebuchadnezzar spake and said unto them, Is it true,
O Shadrach, Meshach, and Abed-nego, do not ye
serve my gods, nor worship the golden image which I
have set up?*

15 *Now if ye be ready that at what time ye hear the
sound of the cornet, flute, harp, sackbut, psaltery, and
dulcimer, and all kinds of music, ye fall down and
worship the image which I have made; well: but if ye*

worship not, ye shall be cast the same hour into the midst of a burning fiery furnace; and who is that God that shall deliver you out of my hands?

16 *Shadrach, Meshach, and Abed-nego, answered and said to the king, O Nebuchadnezzar, we are not careful to answer thee in this matter.*

17 *If it be so, our God whom we serve is able to deliver us from the burning fiery furnace, and he will deliver us out of thine hand, O king.*

18 *But if not, be it known unto thee, O king, that we will not serve thy gods, nor worship the golden image which thou hast set up.*

Spiritual Fortitude

Mission accomplished. When Nebuchadnezzar heard of the acts of the rebellious young Jews, he flew into one of his typical rages, demanding that these alleged traitors be brought before him. But to his credit—and perhaps the first crack in Nebuchadnezzar's becoming more compliant—he asked Shadrach, Meshach, and Abed-nego if they'd really done this dastardly deed, perhaps secretly hoping the report was not true.

> *How many times have we kept our allegiance to Jesus under wraps, saying, along with Peter, "I never knew the man!"?*

King Nebuchadnezzar didn't take the Chaldean's word at

face value. He left the door open for Shadrach, Meshach, and Abed-nego to take the trip out to the plain of Dura again and make amends for their unpatriotic actions—or lack of action. All they would have to do would be drop to their knees when the desert orchestra struck up its opening number once again.

I can almost hear Shadrach, Meshach, and Abed-nego saying, "O king, we really don't want to go out there to Dura again. Because even if we did, we would not bow to the great gold statue. It's not that we don't respect you, it's just that you are not God, and we bow only to God." Spiritual guts! That's the best phrase I can think of. Intestinal fortitude and courage born of spiritual integrity, all of which translated into a resounding, "No, king, we just can't do that." And with their final refusal, they told the king they were prepared to be led into the fiery furnace. We Christians today need to appreciate the resolute spirit of these young men: They were not arrogant before the king. The Hebrews did not equivocate or evade the issue. They spoke their minds as children of God. How many times have we kept our allegiance to Jesus under wraps, saying, along with Peter, "I never knew the man!"? Not so for these young men. They spoke the truth without fear, knowing what would happen if the king refused to change his mind. These three young Hebrews were prepared to abide by the rules, even if it meant suffering as a consequence. Only God knows how many millions of other faithful followers throughout history have gone to their own "fiery furnaces" or "lions' dens" for their faith—including the torture and persecution that continues to exist throughout our world today for all modern-day Shadrachs, Meshachs, and Abed-negos.

The die was now cast. The young Hebrews admitted that they were guilty as charged. They felt no need to justify their position because they knew God would protect and defend them. But note one of the most amazing verses in this entire passage: "But if not, be it known unto thee, O king, that we will not serve thy gods, nor worship the golden image which thou hast set up" (3:18). Imagine the maturity and faith of three young men who could say, "King, even if our God does not deliver us from your fiery furnace, we still will not serve your gods or worship your desert statue. We just will not do it!"

Just One More Miracle, God

They knew their God was a God of miracles, and I'm confident that their minds quickly raced back to how Moses had led the children of Israel through the Red Sea, and how tens of thousands of the children of Israel walked through on dry ground, without one of them dying. If God could do that kind of miracle then, why not another miracle now! Later, the apostle Paul would write in Philippians 1:21, "For to me to live is Christ, and to die is gain." That was the courageous spirit of the three Hebrew teenagers. Each time I read this passage, I'm overwhelmed at the bold faith of Daniel's friends. It's my earnest prayer that you and I would trust our God enough to be just as faithful were we to find ourselves in a similar situation.

> *If God could do that kind of miracle then, why not another miracle now!*

19 *Then was Nebuchadnezzar full of fury, and the form of his visage was changed against Shadrach, Meshach, and Abed-nego: therefore he spake, and commanded that they should heat the furnace one seven times more than it was wont to be heated.*

20 *And he commanded the most mighty men that were in
his army to bind Shadrach, Meshach, and Abednego,
and to cast them into the burning fiery furnace.*

Just like a chameleon, Nebuchadnezzar changed his tune from
the earlier conciliatory "let's give them one more chance" to his
usual uncontrollable rage as he sent the three Hebrew men to
their death in the furnace, now heated seven times hotter than
usual. The king had perhaps expected that the determined
Hebrews would strike a deal. After all, what's a little thing like
bowing down to an image if the only alternative is burning to a
crisp in a furnace? But the king was wrong. Again: Shadrach,
Meshach, and Abed-nego were in no mood for deal-making. I'm
sure those who were eavesdropping on this tense palace discussion also may have expected some form of compromise to
emerge, but there would be no compromise when it came to
things of the living God. Here was a king before whom the
nations trembled, and to whom rulers of the known world will-
ingly gave homage . . . and now three young Jewish upstarts had
the audacity to just say no! The king probably wanted to save
their lives from destruction, but he'd painted himself into a political corner with his incontrovertible decree, a manifesto that was
as immutable as any law of the Medes or the Persians. The king
found himself with no choice but to heat up the furnace.

*144,000 Jewish evangelists
will proclaim the message of
the coming kingdom, and
millions of Jewish and
Gentile converts will somehow
survive, though rejecting the
mark of the beast.*

More Than Just a Bible Story

Again, this is more than biblical history. This is a dramatic picture of Jewish people and Gentile converts. The Bible reminds us that millions will be saved during the Tribulation hour. Revelation 7:14 says, "These are they which came out of great tribulation, and have washed their robes, and made them white in the blood of the Lamb." They will be going through the seven years of Tribulation, which the body of Christ, the Church, escapes via the Rapture (Revelation 4:1). On the other hand, 144,000 Jewish evangelists will proclaim the message of the coming Kingdom, and millions of Jewish and Gentile converts will somehow survive, though rejecting the mark of the beast. So just as Nebuchadnezzar ordered the furnace be made seven times hotter for the three Hebrew children, so the seven-year period of Tribulation will be a hot, volatile period in which millions of God's newly born-again children will be placed in the fire of an anti-God atmosphere. But I repeat—multitudes of Jews and Christians will somehow miraculously survive, though rejecting the mark of the beast (Daniel 12:1; Matthew 25:31–34).

21 *Then these men were bound in their coats, their hosen, and their hats, and their other garments, and were cast into the midst of the burning fiery furnace.*

22 *Therefore because the king's commandment was urgent, and the furnace exceeding hot, the flame of the fire slew those men that took up Shadrach, Meshach, and Abed-nego.*

23 *And these three men, Shadrach, Meshach, and Abednego, fell down bound into the midst of the burning fiery furnace.*

Think of the hottest steel plant furnace you have ever seen. Now imagine the temperature as seven times hotter—an increase of 700 percent. Anger often displays itself in over-statements, and Nebuchadnezzar was furious. A small fire would have sufficed. Heating the furnace twice as hot would have roasted these rebellious spirits, killing them ever so slowly. But true to his volatile nature, Nebuchadnezzar was determined to incinerate them, attempting to show the world that he was in charge . . . and that no God of Israel would be a match for his prowess. This would be one more graphic display of a king's power—and a prediction of the earthly power of the Antichrist to come.

Can you feel the heat? But think also of this: Fire not only purifies gold, but it also gets rid of the dross—the flaws and the alien material that cling to the precious metal. That's why gold is so valuable. It's pure. Unadulterated. Free of foreign matter. It was the same that day when the three Hebrew children were shoved into the furnace. The dross—the "mighty" men of the kingdom commissioned by the king to do the terrible deed—were destroyed the moment they opened the fiery furnace door, while Daniel's friends—wearing highly flammable clothing and bound head to foot—found themselves in for further purification of their lives.

24 *Then Nebuchadnezzar the king was astonied, and rose up in haste, and spake, and said unto his counsellors, Did not we cast three men bound into the midst of the fire? They answered and said unto the king, True, O king.*

25 *He answered and said, Lo, I see four men loose, walking in the midst of the fire, and they have no hurt; and the form of the fourth is like the Son of God.*

26 *Then Nebuchadnezzar came near to the mouth of the burning fiery furnace, and spake, and said, Shadrach, Meshach, and Abed-nego, ye servants of the most high God, come forth, and come hither. Then Shadrach, Meshach, and Abed-nego, came forth of the midst of the fire.*

27 *And the princes, governors, and captains, and the king's counsellors, being gathered together, saw these men, upon whose bodies the fire had no power, nor was an hair of their head singed, neither were their coats changed, nor the smell of fire had passed on them.*

The Fourth Man in the Fire

Nebuchadnezzar didn't retreat to his private quarters to wait for an official report on the demise of the three Hebrew children later in the day. He sat there in rapt attention, eagerly watching what his decree would do to anyone who refused to bow to his image. The king was not prepared for what he was about to encounter. Scripture says that he jumped up, astonished at what he saw. As he did, he asked his high officials what was certainly a logical question: "Didn't we just put three men into the furnace? Why then do I see four men—all unhurt? Are my eyes playing tricks on me? And look . . . no one is bound. Didn't I see you tying them up? Then, why aren't they on fire? This makes no sense. They're still walking around as if nothing happened. But what's really got me confused is that fourth man. Who is he? How did he get in there?"

Perhaps the most telling comment of all comes from the mouth of the king when he says, "the form of the fourth is like the Son of God" (3:25). A more accurate translation of what the king said would be "like a son of the gods." The

Babylonians believed that their gods had progeny, so Nebuchadnezzar was commenting on what he thought was a supernatural being in the fire—the fourth man—a son of one of the Babylonian deities. Still unwilling to admit that the one true God might be involved in this miracle, the king continues to credit pagan deities for this bewildering turn of events.

The King on a Losing Streak

Braving the intense heat, and now bewildered, Nebuchadnezzar approaches the furnace door and personally calls for Shadrach, Meshach, and Abed-nego to come out, addressing them as "servants of the most high God." Has the king come a step closer to believing in this God of the Hebrews? How many miracles—or dream interpretations—will it take for this stubborn king to see the light? It does appear that Nebuchadnezzar is becoming somewhat impressed with the power of the God of Israel—the God, he realizes, who has now overruled his decree, leaving these Jewish boys unscathed. At this moment he must also be rethinking Daniel's prophecy—the dream of the statue that would be pulverized by a rock and encompass the whole earth. The scoreboard in the furnace room now reads:

Three Hebrew Children—1
King—0

The king is on a losing streak. He does not know that the fourth person in the fire is the pre-incarnate Son of God, Jesus Christ. He does not know that Jesus has existed from all eternity—"from everlasting" (Micah 5:2)—and that He is "the mighty God" (Isaiah 9:6).

*We don't have to go through
our fiery furnaces alone.
Jesus says, "I'll go through
them with you."*

Jesus Will Never Leave Us

Jesus Christ is the "Son" from all eternity. So, therefore, it really is no surprise that He should appear as a protector of the three Hebrew children during their ordeal. Christ existed before He came to earth. He truly is from everlasting. He is God, the second member of the Trinity. But how did He appear in the fiery furnace, one asks? By a Christophany, an appearance of Jesus Christ occurring in the Old Testament. And now we see Him, this time in the fiery furnace with three men who'd been faithful to their God. What is the message for you and me in this passage? Simply this: Whatever our trials may be, Jesus is always in our midst, administering comfort to us in our greatest hour of need. Hebrews 13:5 states: "I will never leave thee, nor forsake thee." That's the message for you and me. We don't have to go through our fiery furnaces alone. Jesus says, "I'll go through them with you."

> 28 Then Nebuchadnezzar spake, and said, Blessed be the
> God of Shadrach, Meshach, and Abed-nego, who hath
> sent his angel, and delivered his servants that trusted
> in him, and have changed the king's word, and yielded
> their bodies, that they might not serve nor worship
> any god, except their own God.

> 29 *Therefore I make a decree, That every people, nation,*
> *and language, which speak any thing amiss against the*
> *God of Shadrach, Meshach, and Abed-nego, shall be*
> *cut in pieces, and their houses shall be made a*
> *dunghill: because there is no other God that can deliv-*
> *er after this sort.*
>
> 30 *Then the king promoted Shadrach, Meshach, and*
> *Abed-nego, in the province of Babylon.*

Here, again, God blesses those who are faithful to Him. The king has little choice but to praise God for delivering Shadrach, Meshach, and Abed-nego. He now admits that an angel—which can also be translated "deity"—was sent to deliver them from the furnace. Now King Nebuchadnezzar switches gears again, this time decreeing that anyone who speaks against the great God of Israel shall be cut to pieces, and their houses made into dunghills—a threat, you'll remember, reserved earlier for the wise men and magicians who could not interpret his dream.

The Flaming Flame Will Not Be Quenched

Again, this is more than just a story. The deeper meaning of this passage—and of this entire chapter—is this: During the Tribulation period the false prophet will set up an image of the Antichrist and make people bow to it. If they do not worship the image, they will be put to death. During that same Tribulation period the entire world will become a fiery furnace. Psalm 97:3 says, "A fire goeth before him." Ezekiel 20:47 reads, "The flaming flame shall not be quenched." Zephaniah 1:18 tells us, "The whole land shall be devoured by the fire of his jealousy." Malachi 4:1 reads, "The day cometh, that shall burn as an oven."

The Great Tribulation is going to be a horrendous time for earth's inhabitants. But remember . . . the three Hebrew children went through their fiery trial unscathed. Their clothes were left intact, and not even a hair on their heads was singed. There was no smell of fire or smoke on their bodies—all a dramatic picture of the remnant of Jews who are going to be spared during the Tribulation hour as well as millions of newly converted Christians. God always has, and always will, have a way of protecting His own. There is a terrible time coming. Jeremiah 30:7 says, "Alas! for that day is great, so that none is like it: it is even the time of Jacob's trouble; but he shall be saved out of it." That's the good news. In Daniel 12:1 we also read, "There shall be a time of trouble, such as never was since there was a nation even to that same time: and at that time thy people shall be delivered, every one that shall be found written in the book."

Yes, this will be a time of great difficulty for the Jews. But there are also two great statements of encouragement: "they shall be saved out of it" and "thy people shall be delivered." Jesus said in Matthew 24:22, "And except those days should be shortened, there should no flesh be saved: but for the elect's sake those days shall be shortened." This is a key verse because of the word *elect*. Some Christians believe the Church will be compelled to endure the Tribulation hour because the *elect* are present. But it's important to determine which group of "elect" God has in mind. The elect group mentioned here is that group meeting on the Sabbath day, in synagogues, and fleeing from Judaea to the mountains of Petra. This cannot be a reference to Christians, but rather to the Jewish elect, referred to in Isaiah 42:1, 45:4, 65:9, and 65:22. *Yahweh* is speaking here about His wife Israel. They are going to be spared the wrath of the Tribulation period, and this is what the Hebrew children represent and, essentially, what the entire chapter portrays.

Now, as we move on to chapter four of the Book of Daniel, will we continue to encounter a hostile, volatile King

Nebuchadnezzar? Or will we begin to see some permanent changes in his attitude toward Daniel, Shadrach, Meshach, and Abed-nego and to the one whom he now admits to be the true God? I think you'll be amazed—not only at how the drama unfolds, but how chapter four takes us another step closer to the further unsealing of final end-time mysteries.

The Testimony of a King . . . His Reason Restored

DANIEL 4:1–3

1 *Nebuchadnezzar the king, unto all people, nations, and languages, that dwell in all the earth; Peace be multiplied unto you.*

2 *I thought it good to show the signs and wonders that the high God hath wrought toward me.*

3 *How great are his signs! and how mighty are his wonders! his kingdom is an everlasting kingdom, and his dominion is from generation to generation.*

AFTER THE EVENTS in this chapter occurred, an apparently docile King Nebuchadnezzar issued a proclamation declaring he had finally learned his lesson: that indeed the most high God was in control of a realm greater than his own—a Kingdom that will last eternally, dominating earthly powers for generations to come. This decree was written by the king himself, his regal attempt to tell an entire nation of the great God he had now come to honor and respect.

Nebuchadnezzar's Dream

4 *I Nebuchadnezzar was at rest in mine house, and flourishing in my palace:*

5 I saw a dream which made me afraid, and the thoughts upon my bed and the visions of my head troubled me.

6 Therefore made I a decree to bring in all the wise men of Babylon before me, that they might make known unto me the interpretation of the dream.

7 Then came in the magicians, the astrologers, the Chaldeans, and the soothsayers: and I told the dream before them; but they did not make known unto me the interpretation thereof.

8 But at the last Daniel came in before me, whose name was Belteshazzar, according to the name of my god, and in whom is the spirit of the holy gods: and before him I told the dream, saying,

9 O Belteshazzar, master of the magicians, because I know that the spirit of the holy gods is in thee, and no secret troubleth thee, tell me the visions of my dream that I have seen, and the interpretation thereof.

10 Thus were the visions of mine head in my bed; I saw, and behold a tree in the midst of the earth, and the height thereof was great.

11 The tree grew, and was strong, and the height thereof reached unto heaven, and the sight thereof to the end of all the earth:

12 The leaves thereof were fair, and the fruit thereof much, and in it was meat for all: the beasts of the field had shadow under it, and the fowls of the heaven dwelt in the boughs thereof, and all flesh was fed of it.

13 I saw in the visions of my head upon my bed, and, behold, a watcher and an holy one came down from heaven;

14 *He cried aloud, and said thus, Hew down the tree,*
and cut off his branches, shake off his leaves, and
scatter his fruit: let the beasts get away from under it,
and the fowls from his branches:

15 *Nevertheless leave the stump of his roots in the earth,*
even with a band of iron and brass, in the tender grass
of the field; and let it be wet with the dew of heaven,
and let his portion be with the beasts in the grass of
the earth:

16 *Let his heart be changed from man's, and let a beast's*
heart be given unto him; and let seven times pass over
him.

17 *This matter is by the decree of the watchers, and the*
demand by the word of the holy ones: to the intent
that the living may know that the most High ruleth in
the kingdom of men, and giveth it to whomsoever he
will, and setteth up over it the basest of men.

18 *This dream I king Nebuchadnezzar have seen. Now*
thou, O Belteshazzar, declare the interpretation thereof,
forasmuch as all the wise men of my kingdom are not
able to make known unto me the interpretation: but
thou art able; for the spirit of the holy gods is in thee.

The score would soon be
evened, as we shall see as the
drama of this chapter
unfolds.

We have now arrived at the latter half of the king's reign, and some twenty-three years have passed between chapters three and four. Nebuchadnezzar has been a successful warrior abroad for most of his career, and he is now spending the remainder of his life in relative ease at his palace in Babylon. Chapter four could probably be called Nebuchadnezzar's spiritual biography. But just as leopards are not known for changing their spots, so the king remained a proud man and would later have to pay the price for forcing his subjects to worship his great gold image on the plain of Dura a generation earlier. The score would soon be evened, as we shall see as the drama of this chapter unfolds.

Daniel—Consistent in Courage

Once again, King Nebuchadnezzar had a dream that caused him great anxiety. By now, he seemed convinced that the old guard of magicians, astrologers, and wise men would not have the necessary skills to interpret his latest dream, so he brought in a new group of seers, "all the wise men of Babylon," not just those from the palace. This time, he didn't play games by asking them to tell him his dream and give him the interpretation. He told them the dream immediately. Still, even the wisest in the realm were at a complete loss for an interpretation. I've always wondered why he didn't bring Daniel in immediately instead of going through the frustration of working with supposed wise men who never seemed to be able to deliver. Eventually, Daniel (Belteshazzar) was brought before the king, taken away momentarily from his busy life as judge and prime minister of the realm. Nebuchadnezzar now knew that only a supernatural being could interpret his latest anxiety-ridden dream, and he seemed confident that Daniel was the man to give him the answers he needed.

*He crawled about on his
hands and knees, disheveled,
a mad monarch forced to
eat grass as an animal.*

Trees = Power

As described in the passage above, the king's latest dream was about a luxuriant tree of great height, with branches heavy with enough fruit to sustain the lives of many. But then a holy "watcher" descended from heaven and commanded that the tree be cut down, leaving only a stump in the ground. To a king who was already paranoid about losing his kingdom, this dream was one more in a painful series that indicated neither time nor the God of the Hebrews was on his side. Let's look at this dream and its various components as they relate both to biblical symbolism and to final end-time mysteries.

Throughout the Word of God, trees represent kingdoms and powers. Two examples: 1) The cedar tree usually refers to the nation of Lebanon (1 Kings 4:33) and 2) The fig tree speaks of Israel (Joel 1:7; Hosea 9:10; Matthew 24:32). Nebuchadnezzar did not know it at the time, but the great tree that reached to heaven represented him and his vast empire. Babylon was a powerful tree—a mighty kingdom that had refused to bow its head to anything but a lifeless Marduk and the other Babylonian gods. But it was an abusive power, filled with the pride of an arrogant king who had crafted a golden image and made his subjects bow to it. Because of the king's arrogance, God would cut the tree representing Nebuchadnezzar's great power to the ground, but enough would remain (the stump) to indicate that it was still alive enough to undergo seven years of testing, a graphic picture of the seven-year Tribulation hour—a time we are rapidly approaching.

Twenty-One Judgments

During those seven years of trouble, according to the dream, the king would be stricken down. He crawled about on his hands and knees, disheveled, a mad monarch forced to eat grass as an animal. His hair probably grew to where it touched his back. His fingernails were like bird claws. There was a time when skeptics argued that such a situation was not plausible. Raymond Harrison recited a personal experience with a modern case similar to that of Nebuchadnezzar, which he observed in a British mental institution in 1946. He found a man who was mentally deranged, had claws like a bird, with matted hair hanging all the way to his feet. Furthermore, the man's diet was grass, which he ate while crawling on all fours. The disease was given a name: Boanthropy, or Zoanthropy. Medical records prove this malady does, in fact, exist—and is the same disease, or the equivalent, that Nebuchadnezzar experienced in his dream and life. This state of mental derangement would last for seven years, representing the duration of the Tribulation, that terrible time on earth when millions who insist on honoring a false god will go through judgments destined to inundate the world.

How many judgments will there be during these perilous days? Twenty-one! Each of them is listed in Revelation chapters six to eighteen. Here are just a few: Revelation 6:2 says the Antichrist appears on a white horse; verses 4 to 8 tell us there will be three other riders. The red horse depicts peace being removed from the earth with the cataclysmic judgments of war annihilating one-third of the world's inhabitants; verse 5 says the rider on a black horse causes mass starvation; and verse 8 gives us the dramatic picture of a rider on a pale horse that causes myriads of diseases, eliminating another one-fourth of the human race; in verse 9, we see yet another judgment, where millions are slaughtered for honoring the name of God and for declaring their allegiance to the Lord Jesus Christ; verse 12 speaks of the judgments in the heavens: "And I beheld when he had opened the sixth seal, and, lo, there was a great earthquake; and the sun became black as sackcloth of hair, and the moon became as blood." The judgment described in Revelation 8:1 is so terrible that it unleashes the other fourteen judgments, causing an unusual silence in heaven for about the space of half an hour.

> *There is only one part of the prophecy yet to come: the stone smashing the feet of the image— Christ's glorious return to establish His millennial reign upon the earth (Revelation 20:4).*

The angels, knowing what is coming, are so stunned as they contemplate the future that there is a holy hush in the presence of God. This day is rapidly approaching, and the Book of Daniel is the prophecy through which these end-time mysteries are now being unsealed. In chapter two, we saw the future kingdoms clearly delineated, and now we know that most of Daniel's prophecy has already happened. There is only one part of the prophecy yet to come: the stone smashing the feet of the image— Christ's glorious return to establish His millennial reign for one thousand years upon the earth (Revelation 20:4). This is all going to take place soon. But before it does, there will be the Tribulation period, pictured by the example of a mentally deranged, animal-like king, who crawls on the ground eating grass for seven years. Once again, a desperate king turns to his foreign friend and counselor for the interpretation of his dream. And again, what Daniel is about to tell the king is not good news. But Daniel remains courageous, refusing to dodge the issue. God has given Daniel the interpretation, and he is prepared to speak the mind of God freely before King Nebuchadnezzar.

Daniel's Response to the Dream

19 *Then Daniel, whose name was Belteshazzar, was
astonied for one hour, and his thoughts troubled him.
The king spake, and said, Belteshazzar, let not the
dream, or the interpretation thereof, trouble thee.
Belteshazzar answered and said, My lord, the dream
be to them that hate thee, and the interpretation thereof to thine enemies.*

Even though Daniel had been given divine truth directly from God, it still was not easy for him to express those thoughts to the king. He stood there astonished, virtually unable to speak for one hour. Then we see a small crack in the king's pride as Nebuchadnezzar becomes compassionate toward Daniel, telling him not to let the dream or its interpretation get him down. The king seems to be stiffening his upper lip; since he's been in a similar situation before with Daniel, he's probably gearing himself up to hear an interpretation that may not be favorable. Essentially Daniel says, "O, king, I've got bad news for you." It's always difficult to bring bad tidings to a friend or a colleague, and Daniel, a trusted servant of the king, must have felt great pain in his own heart. Yet, he remained courageous and spoke the Word of God, even though it was a terrible confirmation of what God would do.

Even in a direct one-on-one sit-
uation with the king, Daniel
did not hesitate to say, "Thus
saith the Lord."

Speaking the Truth in Love

Comfortable or not, it is always the role of the believer to speak the truth in love. Just as a doctor is obliged to cut out a cancer if he is to fulfill his role of worthy physician, so we are compelled to speak the truth of God's Word with compassion. God says that we must warn people of the wrath to come, or their blood will be on our hands. It's the same message Paul communicated to young Timothy in 2 Timothy 4:2: "Preach the word; be instant in season, out of season; reprove, rebuke, exhort with all longsuffering and doctrine." This is what Daniel did once again. The prophet of God was not afraid. He had been given a message from God, and he would deliver it. Daniel was prepared to stand firm in his convictions. Even in a direct one-on-one situation with the king, Daniel did not hesitate to say, "Thus saith the Lord."

Daniel's Interpretation of the King's Dream

20 *The tree that thou sawest, which grew, and was*
strong, whose height reached unto the heaven, and the
sight thereof to all the earth;

21 *Whose leaves were fair, and the fruit thereof much,*
and in it was meat for all; under which the beasts of

*the field dwelt, and upon whose branches the fowls of
the heaven had their habitation:*

22 *It is thou, O king, that art grown and become strong:
for thy greatness is grown, and reacheth unto heaven,
and thy dominion to the end of the earth.*

23 *And whereas the king saw a watcher and an holy one
coming down from heaven, and saying, Hew the tree
down, and destroy it; yet leave the stump of the roots
thereof in the earth, even with a band of iron and
brass, in the tender grass of the field; and let it be wet
with the dew of heaven, and let his portion be with
the beasts of the field, till seven times pass over him;*

24 *This is the interpretation, O king, and this is the decree
of the most High, which is come upon my lord the king:*

25 *That they shall drive thee from men, and thy dwelling
shall be with the beasts of the field, and they shall
make thee to eat grass as oxen, and they shall wet
thee with the dew of heaven, and seven times shall
pass over thee, till thou know that the most High
ruleth in the kingdom of men, and giveth it to whomsoever he will.*

26 *And whereas they commanded to leave the stump of the
tree roots; thy kingdom shall be sure unto thee, after
that thou shalt have known that the heavens do rule.*

27 *Wherefore, O king, let my counsel be acceptable unto
thee, and break off thy sins by righteousness, and
thine iniquities by showing mercy to the poor; if it
may be a lengthening of thy tranquillity.*

The first piece of discomforting news for Nebuchadnezzar was that he was, in fact, the tree. It was a big, strong, sturdy tree, providing food and sustenance for all, seemingly invincible. But Daniel's message was that this power could not last forever— a recurring theme, and one you'd think would now be settling deep into the king's heart. As the tree in the dream, Nebuchadnezzar would literally be "cut down to size," with only a stump remaining: alive but ineffective. He would one day be revived, but only after a terrible mental sickness had afflicted him.

Here I must submit that God is not only a God of irony, but also one of considerable humor. You'll recall the passage where Nebuchadnezzar determined to make his great image all gold because he believed that nobody was ever going to defeat him. When he made that decision, he essentially was saying to Daniel, "Look Daniel, I really don't care what you told me about all that gold, silver, bronze, and clay . . . my statue is going to be all gold. Period!" So what does God do as He gives Daniel the interpretation of the tree dream? He says, "By the way, King, I want you to notice something about this tree— which is you. There are a couple of things on the bottom you need to know about, like a little band of brass and iron!" I have a feeling this irony was not lost on the king as he probably said to himself, "Come on, not that brass and iron stuff again!" God was saying, through Daniel, "King, the secret I've revealed to Daniel, which you accepted at the time, is going to happen; whether you like it or not, the 'brass and iron' are still major players in your ultimate demise."

The "Watchers" Among Us—Today!

And who was telling the king about his future? The "watcher" and the "holy one"—angels, sent to do the bidding of their

Father. These watchers see all and tell all—to God. They are all around. They protect you, and they protect me. You'll remember when Jesus was on earth He said, "Thinkest thou that I cannot now pray to my Father, and he shall presently give me more than twelve legions of angels?" (Matthew 26:53). A legion in the Roman army consisted of a group totaling seven thousand soldiers. Hence, twelve times seven thousand, or eighty-four thousand angels, would appear instantaneously at the word of Jesus Christ if He requested help.

These were angels who would come from the "third heaven" (2 Corinthians 12:2). That's so far into space it's mind-boggling. However, here's an attempt to describe the third heaven and the distance God's elect angels travel, coming from that location to earth. The atmosphere, troposphere, stratosphere, mesosphere, ionosphere, and exosphere are all part of the first heaven and reach upwards into the first six hundred miles of space. The second heaven begins at that point and is so astronomical that it's practically impossible to comprehend. Recently astronomers discovered a new quasar some fourteen hundred billion light years from earth. How far is that, you ask? Well, light travels at the rate of 186,000 miles per second. This produces a total of six trillion miles annually and is called a light year. Thus, the second heaven extends upwards into space some fourteen hundred billion times six trillion miles. Beyond that is the third heaven—the heaven of heavens— God's throne. It's from this seemingly immeasurable distance that these "watchers" and "holy ones" brought Nebuchadnezzar his message of doom in the dream.

When we read a detailed history of Nebuchadnezzar's reign, we see how proud the king was of his great accomplishments, among them a nation he had fashioned into a peaceful shelter and granary for all—full of nutritional abundance. Because of his superb administrative abilities, no one in Babylon would go hungry. Now that great tree of plenty would be destroyed . . . and there, again, was this annoying little band of brass and iron.

Here's an interesting footnote of history. Nebuchadnezzar often took his military campaigns into the great forests and woods of Lebanon and had become infatuated by the great cedars there. We also read that the king so loved the cedars of Lebanon that he cut many of them down with his own hands. Now that which the king loved would be cut to a mere stump in the ground, meaning that he would soon be removed from office and forced to live away from the palace as a mentally incompetent vagabond, scratching the earth for food as an animal. How long would he be forced to live like this? Until he acknowledged that the true God in heaven was sovereign ruler over the kingdoms of earth.

> *There would be no promise of escape from the wrath to come without repentance.*

An Invitation Is Extended

As any good preacher would do after a powerful sermon or illustration, Daniel gave his friend the king an opportunity to repent of his evil ways. Up to that time, Nebuchadnezzar had been immensely cruel to thousands of his subjects, especially during his massive building campaigns (Habakkuk 2:11–13). So, Daniel did not flinch on his interpretation of the dream. There would be no promise that the king would escape from the wrath to come. But Daniel did indicate that perhaps—just maybe—almighty God might extend the king's era of tranquillity if he would repent of his terrible acts of oppression, engage in acts of righteousness, and demonstrate a greater degree of mercy to the poor in Babylon.

The Realization of the Dream

28 *All this came upon the king Nebuchadnezzar.*

29 *At the end of twelve months he walked in the palace of the kingdom of Babylon.*

30 *The king spake, and said, Is not this great Babylon, that I have built for the house of the kingdom by the might of my power, and for the honour of my majesty?*

31 *While the word was in the king's mouth, there fell a voice from heaven, saying, O king Nebuchadnezzar, to thee it is spoken; The kingdom is departed from thee.*

32 *And they shall drive thee from men, and thy dwelling shall be with the beasts of the field: they shall make thee to eat grass as oxen, and seven times shall pass over thee, until thou know that the most High ruleth in the kingdom of men, and giveth it to whomsoever he will.*

33 *The same hour was the thing fulfilled upon Nebuchadnezzar: and he was driven from men, and did eat grass as oxen, and his body was wet with the dew of heaven, till his hairs were grown like eagles' feathers, and his nails like birds' claws.*

It's now a year later, and God has been patient with Nebuchadnezzar. Despite his earlier bent toward believing in the God of the Hebrews, the king remained stubborn, pretending he was an earthly ruler who would reign forever. Even as he hoped that his friend Daniel would be wrong, the prophecy began to be fulfilled. At the tragic moment when the king finds himself on the verge of a mental breakdown, he begins to engage in a sort of lonely soliloquy about his exploits as ruler of Babylon. He was probably strolling on the roof of his palace as he spoke—grounds that covered a six-mile area—surveying his great city and all that he had done to make it one of the ancient wonders. His royal chest filled with pride as he boasted of accomplishments never done by others. Yes, he had done some amazing things and was undoubtedly the greatest kingdom builder in ancient times. He had built two enormous temples and seventeen ornate religious shrines. His Hanging Gardens of Babylon were without equal, something the Greeks later declared one of the Seven Wonders of the World. He had constructed the famous Ishtar Gate—magnificent with its carved bulls and four-legged dragons etched in high relief. With the assistance of hand-picked engineers, he had designed and created amazingly intricate hydraulic systems that carried water effortlessly up from the Euphrates River to his gardens high above the city—gardens that housed some of the most exotic plants and trees of his day.

But as he reveled in his kingly accomplishments, the voice from heaven finally came, even as Daniel had prophesied one year earlier. The words of the watcher were, "O king . . . the kingdom is departed from thee" (4:31). It was finally over. Payday had arrived. At that moment, the king realized even the best laid plans of kings and men are as dust. The mills of God may grind slowly, but they grind exceedingly fine. Surely and firmly judgment falls when people refuse to glorify God by taking full credit for their worldly accomplishments. Again, this is the scenario of the seven-year Tribulation period—a time in history when the greatest sin will be committed by another king—the infamous Antichrist, who will magnify himself above God (Daniel 11:36). God despises and judges such arrogance. That's why Proverbs 16:18 declares, "Pride goeth before destruction, and an haughty spirit before a fall."

The Message of a Frog

As I was preparing this chapter I reminded my wife, Rexella, of a little story that speaks straight to this issue of pride. Once there was a little frog sitting on the ground. He watched forlornly as he saw the great birds of the sky flying overhead. *Oh, if I could only fly like the eagles I would be extremely happy,* he thought. Well, one day, two of the eagles were on the ground. The frog approached them, saying, "Say, I wonder if you two fellows would do me a favor. I've got this long stick, and if you'd just put it in your beaks, I could hang on to it, and we could fly through space together. I've always wanted to fly."

The eagles agreed to the strange request, and slowly they lifted the frog from the comfort of his lily pad, up into the unfamiliar but exhilarating sky above, the frog hanging on to the stick for dear life. Before long, the other frogs turned their heads skyward and in disbelief—unable to see the stick—saw their little green friend ascending farther and farther into space. His friends on the ground began to praise this stunt saying, "What genius thought of doing this?" The frog's ego at this point got the best of him when he shouted, "I-I-I did." By doing so he lost his biting grip on the stick and plunged to earth in a humiliating landing.

My friend, we can do absolutely nothing on our own—no more than that frog could fly without some help from his friends. All we do and have are gifts from God. So the next time you are tempted to say, "I did it all on my own," I hope you'll remember the story of the frog—and that you'll then quickly recall the pride of Nebuchadnezzar, a man who had accomplished great feats to make a name for himself but who, in the process, refused to give God the credit. As a result, he paid the price. He fell, even as Satan did, through pride (1 Timothy 3:6).

Nebuchadnezzar's Response to the Message of the "Watcher"

34 *And at the end of the days I Nebuchadnezzar lifted up mine eyes unto heaven, and mine understanding returned unto me, and I blessed the most High, and I praised and honoured him that liveth for ever, whose dominion is an everlasting dominion, and his kingdom is from generation to generation:*

35 *And all the inhabitants of the earth are reputed as nothing: and he doeth according to his will in the army of heaven, and among the inhabitants of the earth: and none can stay his hand, or say unto him, What doest thou?*

36 *At the same time my reason returned unto me; and for the glory of my kingdom, mine honour and brightness returned unto me; and my counsellors and my lords sought unto me; and I was established in my kingdom, and excellent majesty was added unto me.*

37 *Now I Nebuchadnezzar praise and extol and honour the King of heaven, all whose works are truth, and his ways judgment: and those that walk in pride he is able to abase.*

> *It took the sickness of a*
> *deranged mind to bring him*
> *to his senses, and what a con-*
> *version experience he had.*

His reason now restored after his period of derangement, King Nebuchadnezzar swallowed his pride and raised his humbled eyes toward heaven. After his terrible experience as a mad monarch scratching out an existence as an animal, now he was finally willing to honor the true King of heaven. He recognized that all God's works were true and that those who live out their days in pride will be humbled beyond recognition.

What brought Nebuchadnezzar to this realization? It wasn't a miracle. When he saw the Hebrew children in the fiery furnace without a hair singed or a piece of clothing carrying the smell of smoke, and the fourth man in the furnace with them, and their walking out unscathed—that didn't make him a believer. In Nebuchadnezzar's case, it took the sickness of a deranged mind to bring him to his senses, and what a conversion experience he had. The truth we have seen again and again in this chapter is highlighted in Paul's writing to the church at Rome: "But God be thanked, that ye were the servants of sin, but ye have obeyed from the heart that form of doctrine which was delivered you" (Romans 6:17). The message? There is hope for all.

In 1 Corinthians 6:9–10, we read, "Know ye not that the unrighteous shall not inherit the kingdom of God? Be not deceived: neither fornicators, nor idolaters, nor adulterers, nor effeminate, nor abusers of themselves with mankind, Nor thieves, nor covetous, nor drunkards, nor revilers, nor extortioners, shall inherit the kingdom of God." But praise God, the apostle doesn't stop there. In verse 11 Paul continues, "And such were some of you: but ye are washed, but ye are sanctified, but ye are justified in the name of the Lord Jesus, and by the Spirit of our God."

The good news is always followed by even better news, that none of us needs to be what we once were. There is hope for us all—just as there was hope and an opportunity for restitution for King Nebuchadnezzar. Yes, he paid a great price for his transgressions, just as you and I will always pay a heavy toll when we turn our backs on the foundational principles that God has ordained. True repentance means turning "about face" and heading in God's direction. When we do this, we no longer will want to do the evil we once did. Now, after all the fighting, kicking, and screaming Nebuchadnezzar did to distance himself from the one true God, he finally realized that he was the problem, and that his own sinful pride was the issue. It took crawling around as an animal for a year to make him realize that he needed to square himself away with the true God. Nebuchadnezzar's conversion changed him from the inside out. Yes, it's a great, historically accurate story. But the deeper, underlying message of Nebuchadnezzar's narrative— and his dream—is that this is all simply a precursor of the shattering events yet to come: seven years of Tribulation where unbridled humans will set themselves up as New Age gods, living unholy, prideful lives and worshipping seducing spirits, even when the obvious handwriting of warning begins to appear on the wall—the intriguing story and subject of chapter five.

❖5❖

Don't Look Now, but There's Something on Your Wall

DANIEL 5:1–4

1 Belshazzar the king made a great feast to a thousand of his lords, and drank wine before the thousand.

2 Belshazzar, whiles he tasted the wine, commanded to bring the golden and silver vessels which his father Nebuchadnezzar had taken out of the temple which was in Jerusalem; that the king, and his princes, his wives, and his concubines, might drink therein.

3 Then they brought the golden vessels that were taken out of the temple of the house of God which was at Jerusalem; and the king, and his princes, his wives, and his concubines, drank in them.

4 They drank wine, and praised the gods of gold, and of silver, of brass, of iron, of wood, and of stone.

ANOTHER TITLE FOR this chapter could be "The World's Wildest Party," hosted by playboy millionaire Belshazzar, grandson of Nebuchadnezzar, and number two in command in Babylon. It was a drunken orgy where the women were in abundance and the wine flowed like water—a graphic example of "Eat, drink, and be merry, for tomorrow we die." With one small correction: They would not die tomorrow; they would be attacked, defeated, and murdered that very night by stealthy troops already assembled deep beneath the city.

Before we slip into the celebration to see what was really going on, let's look at the man Belshazzar. Who was he? What were his credentials? It's important to note that for many years, liberal interpreters of Holy Writ pleaded their case that there was no such person at all. Scholar Ferdinand Hitzack, in 1850, said that no one by the name of Belshazzar had ever existed, and therefore the Book of Daniel was a farce. However, just four years later, J. G. Taylor was on an archeological dig in southern Iraq where he dug up artifacts that contained sixty lines of cuneiform—a system of writing used for a number of ancient Near Eastern languages from c. 3000 B.C. until the first century A.D. Primarily a Mesopotamian system, cuneiform was inscribed on clay, stone, metal, and other hard materials. This was a key discovery for Taylor and the Christian world, because one of those sixty lines of cuneiform prayed for the health of Nabonidus, and his son Belshazzar. In 1924, Sidney Smith did some excavating of his own in the region and he, too, unearthed an artifact that stated Nabonidus gave the kingship to his son Belshazzar. Again, liberal Bible scholars do not have a position at all. In fact, those who wish to appear foolish need only to suggest that the Bible has errors in content, history, or personnel. The answers may not be immediately observable, but the truth will always emerge, even as it did in the case of Belshazzar, whom some say was a phantom.

*When the cat's away we
know what the mice do: They
play and play and play—as
if there were no tomorrow.*

Nabonidus was a great military warrior, always away on a mission to add territory and subjects to his mighty Babylon, and always returning with the booty and spoils of the conquered. In his absence, Babylon was left in the control of his son, Belshazzar. And when the cat's away, we know what the mice do: They play and play and play—as if there were no tomorrow. And that's where we pick up our story—and perhaps the wildest party ever held in Babylon. This was no little soiree in a small drawing room with a few guests. The hall for the festivities was enormous—176 feet long and 56 feet wide. Some of the dinners held in that room had as many as ten thousand guests, with the largest banquet in history having an invitation list of 69,800 people. That's a lot of folks, and I'm sure that much of the celebration had to be celebrated outdoors. This is the enormous physical environment of chapter five. Big party. Big spenders. Big orgy. Big trouble!

The problems started when young Belshazzar made the mistake of using the holy vessels that his grandfather Nebuchadnezzar stole from the temple in Jerusalem. As far as we know, Nebuchadnezzar committed no sacrilege with these hallowed temple vessels—to his credit. But Belshazzar? He could not have cared less. He wanted to drink, and he didn't care into what kind of cup his servants poured the brew. Imagine the scene: Young Belshazzar is in charge of the affairs of state, but tonight he figures it's time to have a party. He goes over the guest list, and probably says, "Well, with Dad out of the country on another campaign, this is my night to howl." And howl he did, starting by desecrating the Jewish temple vessels—goblets that told the story of God's redemption through blood. Hebrews 9:22 says, "Without shedding of blood is no remission [of sins]." The Jews also believed that blood makes an atonement for sins (Leviticus 17:11). These were holy utensils, not everyday cups and saucers. But Belshazzar ordered them to be filled with booze of all descriptions, much to the delight of his pagan friends who drank, laughed, and danced the night away. But no party lasts forever, and this one would be especially short-lived. Belshazzar would pay dearly for his sacrilege.

Booze was about to become a problem for the young ruler. Have you noticed in the age in which you and I live, that liquor is no less a problem? More than half of all our automobile accidents are alcohol-related. Booze has destroyed more families than anyone can imagine. Drinking has ruined careers, crippled relationships, and left otherwise sane people mentally incompetent. The warnings about alcohol have been in the Bible for thousands of years, and I think it's important to quote a few verses to indicate what God thinks about the issue.

> *During this orgy, God was watching the scene from the portals of heaven, and He was not pleased.*

What God Says about Strong Drink

Proverbs 20:1 says, "Wine is a mocker, strong drink is raging:

and whosoever is deceived thereby is not wise." Proverbs 23:29 reads, "Who hath woe? who hath sorrow? who hath contentions? who hath babbling? who hath wounds without cause? who hath redness of eyes? They that tarry long at the wine; they that go to seek mixed wine." That's why Proverbs 31 commands: "Look not on the wine when it is red." Juice was called wine. The writer of Proverbs said that when the wine turns red and ferments, don't look at it! It's also the message of Proverbs 23:20, "Be not among wine bibbers [drinkers]." Habakkuk 2:15 says, "Woe unto him that giveth his neighbour drink, that puttest thy bottle to him, and makest him drunken also." The judgment of God is upon those who drink, upon those who get drunk, and equally, upon those who serve strong drink to others to get them intoxicated. First Corinthians 6:9–10 and Galatians 5:19–21 state that no drunkard can enter the kingdom of heaven unless he repents of this sin and turns to God.

Well, with that fusillade of verses on what God thinks about wine and strong drink, we note that Belshazzar was not only inebriated as he sat there on his elevated platform, surrounded by his many concubines who encouraged all-night drinking bouts with the guests, but he also added sacrilege to indignity by drinking his kingly brew out of precious vessels of redemption—goblets and temple-ware that represented eternal salvation. To top it off, he and his guests "drank wine, and praised the gods of gold, and of silver, of brass, of iron, of wood, and of stone" (Daniel 5:4). During this orgy, God was watching the scene from the portals of heaven, and He was not pleased.

The Handwriting on the Wall

> 5 *In the same hour came forth fingers of a man's hand,*
> *and wrote over against the candlestick upon the plaster*
> *of the wall of the king's palace: and the king saw the*
> *part of the hand that wrote.*

6 *Then the king's countenance was changed, and his thoughts troubled him, so that the joints of his loins were loosed, and his knees smote one against another.*

7 *The king cried aloud to bring in the astrologers, the Chaldeans, and the soothsayers. And the king spake, and said to the wise men of Babylon, Whosoever shall read this writing, and show me the interpretation thereof, shall be clothed with scarlet, and have a chain of gold about his neck, and shall be the third ruler in the kingdom.*

8 *Then came in all the king's wise men: but they could not read the writing, nor make known to the king the interpretation thereof.*

9 *Then was king Belshazzar greatly troubled, and his countenance was changed in him, and his lords were astonied.*

What would you have done if you'd come to the king's palace for a night of revelry and debauchery and all of a sudden God crashed your party? I have a feeling that most of the guests were so blitzed that they may have thought they were seeing things. Some probably thought, "This is cool . . . look . . . a hand writing on the wall. This Belshazzar guy really knows how to promote magical entertainment. Wow, we didn't know we were going to have a night of illusions to accompany the wine." But Belshazzar had not arranged this particular distraction, and, apparently, he had enough of his wits about him to call the party to an unceremonious halt as the disembodied hand appeared and began writing a message on the plaster wall. The message was clearly written—a warning of the judgment to come because of the desecration of the temple utensils designed to honor *Yahweh,* the God of heaven. The King James version says that "his knees smote one against another" (5:6). That means Belshazzar was so scared that his knees were knocking. The party was now history, and Belshazzar probably wasn't the only one who wished it had ended an hour earlier. The passage says he was pale. I imagine that you and I would have turned a strong shade of white also.

So once again, the wise men were summoned. This time, not to interpret a dream, but to attempt to analyze this disembodied hand writing on the wall. I imagine the sorcerers and magicians may have said among themselves, "Belshazzar's drunk again and is only hallucinating." However, as the soothsayers entered the dining hall, they were stumped because the handwritten message was inscribed indelibly on the wall. Furthermore, they didn't know how to interpret what they were seeing. That's when panic set in, that is, until the queen mother, the wife of Nebuchadnezzar, stepped forward and reminded Belshazzar about a man named Daniel in the kingdom who was pretty good at figuring out this sort of thing.

The Queen Mother Remembers Daniel

10 *Now the queen, by reason of the words of the king
   and his lords, came into the banquet house: and the
   queen spake and said, O king, live for ever: let not thy
   thoughts trouble thee, nor let thy countenance be
   changed:*

11 *There is a man in thy kingdom, in whom is the spirit
   of the holy gods; and in the days of thy father light
   and understanding and wisdom, like the wisdom of*

> *the gods, was found in him; whom the king*
> *Nebuchadnezzar thy father, the king, I say, thy father,*
> *made master of the magicians, astrologers, Chaldeans,*
> *and soothsayers;*
>
> 12 *Forasmuch as an excellent spirit, and knowledge, and*
> *understanding, interpreting of dreams, and showing of*
> *hard sentences, and dissolving of doubts, were found*
> *in the same Daniel, whom the king named*
> *Belteshazzar: now let Daniel be called, and he will*
> *show the interpretation.*

The queen mother is basically saying, "You'd better listen to Daniel because your grandfather really lifted him up, respected him, and used him on more than one occasion to handle situations like this." She knew that Daniel had "the spirit of the holy gods" in and upon him and because of it had the answers. Daniel was around seventeen years old when he was first brought to Babylon from Jerusalem, and now he was approaching his mid-eighties. During this entire time in captivity he kept the power of the Holy Spirit on him—and the queen mother knew it. How did Daniel keep this power upon him during his years of service in Babylon? By spending time in God's precious Book. Daniel knew the Scriptures, and remained profoundly touched by God's Word in the pagan land to which he had been brought so many years earlier. Later, Peter would write in 1 Peter 2:2, "As newborn babes, desire the sincere milk of the word, that ye may grow thereby." That was Daniel's secret then, and it is the source of our strength today as we move swiftly to the end of the age and to the final unsealing of the end-time mysteries. Daniel lived on his knees before God, and when one lives like that—from teenage years to becoming a senior citizen—that person will be such a Spirit-filled being that even the enemies of God will sit up and take notice. Daniel understood the secret of life, and therefore, whenever called on to speak God's truth to a perverse generation of Babylonians, he was ready with a fitting—and correct—word from God. Is Daniel your model today?

Daniel Comes before Belshazzar

13 *Then was Daniel brought in before the king. And the king spake and said unto Daniel, Art thou that Daniel, which art of the children of the captivity of Judah, whom the king my father brought out of Jewry?*

14 *I have even heard of thee, that the spirit of the gods is in thee, and that light and understanding and excellent wisdom is found in thee.*

15 *And now the wise men, the astrologers, have been brought in before me, that they should read this writing, and make known unto me the interpretation thereof: but they could not show the interpretation of the thing:*

16 *And I have heard of thee, that thou canst make interpretations, and dissolve doubts: now if thou canst read the writing, and make known to me the interpretation thereof, thou shalt be clothed with scarlet, and have a chain of gold about thy neck, and shalt be the third ruler in the kingdom.*

> *He knew who he was and whose*
> *he was. He could not have cared*
> *less about the king's offer of a*
> *purple robe and a gold chain.*
> *What value were such temporal*
> *rewards to him?*

By now, I'm sure the party had come to a screeching halt—and I would think more than a few of the guests had sobered up rather quickly. Who wouldn't—a disembodied hand writing on a plaster wall has that effect on party animals. They probably called him killjoy Daniel. But this senior citizen was just as sharp and alert as the day he was spirited away from Jerusalem to Babylon with the other Jewish captives. He knew who he was and Whose he was. He could not have cared less about the king's offer of a purple robe and a gold chain. What value were such temporal rewards to him?

As modern Christians, it seems that we often get confused on this issue. We all like to be rewarded for the good things we do, often asking, *How much am I going to get for doing this? Who's going to notice me if I do this good deed?* But this is not the way of Christ. Hebrews 13:5 says, "Let your conversation be without covetousness; and be content with such things as ye have: for he hath said, I will never leave thee, nor forsake thee." This is the spirit we must maintain during this end-time hour, but it is not the present spirit of Christendom. If one were to study any Bible concordance on adultery, fornication, or licentiousness, and then look up the word *covetousness*—he would discover that immorality and materialism run neck and neck. They are that close in God's sight. God hates the sin of loving money and an obsession with material possessions as much as He hates the sin of immorality.

Daniel Admonishes the Young Ruler

17 *Then Daniel answered and said before the king, Let thy gifts be to thyself, and give thy rewards to another; yet I will read the writing unto the king, and make known to him the interpretation.*

18 *O thou king, the most high God gave Nebuchadnezzar thy father a kingdom, and majesty, and glory, and honour:*

19 *And for the majesty that he gave him, all people, nations, and languages, trembled and feared before him: whom he would he slew; and whom he would he kept alive; and whom he would he set up; and whom he would he put down.*

20 *But when his heart was lifted up, and his mind hardened in pride, he was deposed from his kingly throne, and they took his glory from him:*

21 *And he was driven from the sons of men; and his heart was made like the beasts, and his dwelling was with the wild asses: they fed him with grass like oxen, and his body was wet with the dew of heaven; till he knew that the most high God ruled in the kingdom of men, and that he appointeth over it whomsoever he will.*

22 *And thou his son, O Belshazzar, hast not humbled thine heart, though thou knewest all this;*

23 *But hast lifted up thyself against the Lord of heaven; and they have brought the vessels of his house before thee, and thou, and thy lords, thy wives, and thy concubines, have drunk wine in them; and thou hast praised the gods of silver, and gold, of brass, iron,*

wood, and stone, which see not, nor hear, nor know:
and the God in whose hand thy breath is, and whose
are all thy ways, hast thou not glorified:

24 *Then was the part of the hand sent from him; and this*
writing was written.

Now, after waiting for Belshazzar to stop talking—probably babbling out of sheer nervousness—Daniel begins to speak. I can see him in my mind's eye: strong, erect, courageous, with all of Belshazzar's guests wondering what on earth is happening. This was supposed to be a fun evening at the palace. But instead, it had become "sermon time," and Daniel took advantage of his captive audience by talking about his relationship with Belshazzar's grandfather, Nebuchadnezzar. He was giving Belshazzar a refresher course in the life of the former king. He pulled no punches. There was no revisionist history here. Daniel told it like it was, and his poignant message was: "Nebuchadnezzar genuinely learned his lesson when one day he called on the only true God for mercy. But you, young man, have not yet gotten up to speed, and you're going to pay big time for throwing this wild orgy and for desecrating the sacred utensils set apart for temple worship." This was the sermon to an unhumbled heart, addressed to a man who was drinking out of God-honoring vessels to gods that could neither see nor hear. That's what idolatry was all about then, and that's what worshipping other gods is about today.

God Versus the Gods

King David said in Psalm 115:4–8, "Their idols are silver and gold, the work of men's hands. They have mouths, but they speak not: eyes have they, but they see not: They have ears, but they hear not: noses have they, but they smell not: They have hands, but they handle not: feet have they, but they walk not: neither speak they through their throat. They that make them are like unto them; so is every one that trusteth in them." Daniel is saying the same thing to Belshazzar: "Look, it's just a piece of wood covered with some metal. You made it with your hands. It can't see, hear, talk, move . . . and yet you worship it. Won't you learn from the example of your grandfather, Nebuchadnezzar? He paid a terrible price, eating grass like an animal and wandering around insane. But even after knowing this story, you still remain unconvinced of God's power. Because of your unbelief, you took the vessels from God's house and made a mockery of the utensils representing redemption."

Shame on You, Belshazzar!

I'd call that an earful, and Belshazzar had little choice but to sit there and listen patiently to Daniel's lecture. But the prophet wasn't finished with his scolding. He concluded by saying that the young ruler, too, would pay a dreadful price for his wicked, reprehensible deeds, because God promises to bring every work into judgment (Ecclesiastes 12:14).

Daniel Interprets the Handwriting

25 *And this is the writing that was written, MENE, MENE, TEKEL, UPHARSIN.*

26 *This is the interpretation of the thing: MENE; God hath numbered thy kingdom, and finished it.*

27 *TEKEL; Thou art weighed in the balances, and art found wanting.*

28 *PERES; Thy kingdom is divided, and given to the Medes and Persians.*

Take another snapshot of the occasion. The party revelers have slowed down. No more dancing or drinking at the moment. The orchestra has played its last tune, and the cavernous hall is now silent as Belshazzar and his guests wait for Daniel's interpretation of the words written on the wall by a disembodied hand, words which in Aramaic appeared as *Mene, Mene, Tekel, Upharsin.* The reason for repeating the word *Mene*—"your days are numbered"—is that the Medes and the Persians were, at that very moment, waiting to make their move into the city to subdue it, so there was a *Mene* for each one—one for the Medes, and one for the Persians. They were already assembling beneath the city walls, gathering for the attack, just as God predicted the event on a plaster wall for all at the party to see.

Then Daniel turned to the word *Tekel*—meaning "you are weighed in the balances, and are found wanting." Belshazzar was lacking in everything: in morals, in integrity, and in the fear of God. He had done nothing to honor or glorify the one true God. Here, God engages in the kind of irony He so often has used in the Book of Daniel by changing the word *Upharsin* to *Peres*—just a few vowels away from the word Persia. He said that not only will the kingdom of Belshazzar be divided, but right at this moment, one of those enemies—Persia—was but a spear's throw away. While the foolish young ruler and his irreverent guests had been drinking themselves into oblivion, the "predicted ones" were almost in the hall, weapons poised to murder the brash young ruler.

Belshazzar's Response

> 29 *Then commanded Belshazzar, and they clothed Daniel*
> *with scarlet, and put a chain of gold about his neck,*
> *and made a proclamation concerning him, that he*
> *should be the third ruler in the kingdom.*

30 *In that night was Belshazzar the king of the
Chaldeans slain.*

31 *And Darius the Median took the kingdom, being
about threescore and two years old.*

> **The two enemies of Babylon
> got their heads together and
> figured out a way to enter—
> and capture—the city.**

It was a Babylonian Pearl Harbor. A sneak attack. Just as
American soldiers would be ill-prepared on that fateful day in
Honolulu on December 7, 1941, so great a devastation was
about to come to Babylon. How the two great armies made their
way into the city is a military stratagem worthy of explanation.

Here's how the Medes and Persians won the day. Babylon
was built on the Euphrates River, with a huge wall-like fort sur-
rounding it. It was so formidable that no one could scale it. To
ensure even greater security, the moats around the walls were
filled with water, so enemies would have to swim across and
through those deep waters if they were to have any chance at
approaching the city wall. With these precautions firmly in
place, the Babylonians lived with a strong sense of security. But
they didn't count on the military cunning of the Medes and the
Persians under their rulers, Darius and Cyrus. The two enemies
of Babylon put their heads together and figured out a way to
enter—and capture—the city. First, they blocked off the flow of
the Euphrates River until the water around the city dried up.
They then waited until the moat was dry, stepped into it, dug a

trench under the wall, and in full battle gear marched through the underground canals into the city—while Belshazzar's orgy was in full swing. It was an enormous military success. That night—only moments after the handwriting had appeared on the plaster wall—the troops entered the hall and killed Belshazzar.

This story has given rise to some compelling verse by an unknown poet who has written:

Babylon

Pause in this desert! Here, men say, of old
Belshazzar reigned, and drank from cups of gold;
Here, to his hideous idols, bowed the slave,
And here—God struck him dead!
Where lies his grave?
'Tis lost! —His brazen gates? His soaring towers,
From whose dark tops men watch the starry hours?
All to the dust gone down! The desert bare
Scarce yields an echo when we question "Where?"
The lonely herdsman seeks in vain the spot;
And the black wandering Arab knows it not.
No brick, no fragment, lingers now, to tell
Where Babylon (mighty city!) rose—and fell!
O City, vast and old!
Where, where is thy grandeur fled?
The stream that around thee rolled
Still rolls in its ancient bed!
But where, oh, where art thou gone?
O Babylon! O Babylon!

The giant, when he dies,
Still leaveth his bones behind,

To shrink in the winter skies,
And whiten beneath the wind!
But where, oh, where art thou gone?
O Babylon! O Babylon!

Tho liv'st!—for thy name still glows,
A light in the desert skies;
As the fame of the hero grows
Thrice trebled because he dies!
But where, oh, where art thou gone?
O Babylon! O Babylon!

Before the attack, Daniel was rewarded with his promised clothes of scarlet and gold jewelry, but Belshazzar had little time to enjoy the presentation. God's judgment on the wickedness of the young ruler was swift and complete, and Darius the Mede took the kingdom at sixty-two years of age. It was the end of an era—as Daniel had prophesied years before to Belshazzar's grandfather.

But our story is not yet half told. There is still more excitement and palace intrigue to come as we see a devilish plot developing to destroy Daniel, even as he continues to pray fearlessly at his open window to the God of the Hebrews. Daniel, courageous under any Babylonian administration, remained brave and in full compliance with the laws of his God, even when it meant being thrown unjustly into a den of hungry lions. This kind of spiritual courage eventually led him to the ultimate in prosperity, the engaging subject of chapter six.

⁊·**6**·⁊

Preferred above Princes ... But Not without Lions

DANIEL 6:1–3

1 It pleased Darius to set over the kingdom an hundred
  and twenty princes, which should be over the whole
  kingdom;

2 And over these three presidents; of whom Daniel was
  first: that the princes might give accounts unto them,
  and the king should have no damage.

3 Then this Daniel was preferred above the presidents
  and princes, because an excellent spirit was in him;
  and the king thought to set him over the whole realm.

RECENTLY, I WAS TELLING a friend that I was going to do
a major exposition on the Book of Daniel, and he said,
"Oh, that's about Daniel in the lion's den." I replied,
"Yes, but there's much more to the book than that." It appears
that just about everyone knows this story. Unfortunately, for
many, that's all they know about this mysterious book that provides information on multiplied end-time events that only now, in
our generation, are being unsealed—something we'll investigate
in greater depth when analyzing chapters seven through twelve.

But we're getting a bit ahead of our story. First, some background. Daniel had now served under six administrations as a faithful, wise, competent counselor—all the more remarkable since he was a Jew, a member of that reluctant group of captives brought from Jerusalem to Babylon, and one who never really fit into this foreign culture. Daniel was a survivor because God gave him the strength and the courage to stand up for his faith. And now, in chapter six, we're going to see that strength tested once again.

> *God always sets up those He wants elevated. God had a plan for Daniel's life, and now even the new kings—Darius and Cyrus—find themselves appreciating Daniel and his administrative abilities.*

For anyone to serve six political administrations is a tremendous feat. That's one of many reasons I admire Dr. Billy Graham and the enormous respect he has earned as counselor and friend to six United States presidents. That's a long, impressive history of relationships with our nation's top leaders. It was also a long time for Daniel. For this man of God it had all started with the reign of Nebuchadnezzar, who ultimately lost his kingdom when Babylon was handed over to the Medes and the Persians that fateful night when Belshazzar was preoccupied with wine, women, and song. Then the handwriting began to appear on the wall and the Medo-Persian conquest occurred as the new leaders immediately executed three thousand political prisoners, including all of Babylon's princes and presidents. However, as you'll recall, at the last moment of his life, Belshazzar made Daniel the third in command. Imagine this scenario if you were Darius or Cyrus, leaders of the Medes and the Persians: You conquer a nation, rape and pillage virtually everyone and everything in sight, you kill all the country's key leaders—yet despite your best efforts at assuming complete control, there is still this person, Daniel, who is number three in the kingdom—and who seemingly can't be eliminated. Why wasn't he killed with the others? Why was Daniel, of all people, left to survive and to become a nuisance to the new administration? The only answer I can give is that God always sets up those He wants elevated. God had a plan for Daniel's life, and now even the new kings—Darius and Cyrus—find themselves appreciating Daniel and his administrative abilities, so much so that they make him a president in their kingdom. So, Daniel was one of the three appointed heads of state—at eighty-five years of age.

Jealousy Becomes Treachery

4 Then the presidents and princes sought to find occasion against Daniel concerning the kingdom; but they could find none occasion nor fault; forasmuch as he was faithful, neither was there any error or fault found in him.

5 Then said these men, We shall not find any occasion against this Daniel, except we find it against him concerning the law of his God.

6 Then these presidents and princes assembled together to the king, and said thus unto him, King Darius, live for ever.

7 *All the presidents of the kingdom, the governors, and*
the princes, the counsellors, and the captains, have
consulted together to establish a royal statute, and to
make a firm decree, that whosoever shall ask a peti-
tion of any God or man for thirty days, save of thee,
O king, he shall be cast into the den of lions.

8 *Now, O king, establish the decree, and sign the writ-*
ing, that it be not changed, according to the law of
the Medes and Persians, which altereth not.

9 *Wherefore king Darius signed the writing and the*
decree.

In actions that demonstrated the depth of their anti-
Semitism, the Gentile administrators compelled to work with
Daniel were determined to find a way to put this man down
once and for all. How could they tolerate the presence of a Jew
in such a high position—one greater than their own? That was
the rub. So they pulled Daniel's file. I can just see them scour-
ing the official records looking for just one act of impropriety,
for some minute administrative error. Perhaps they'd find that
some unaccounted for, under-the-table money had changed
hands. Perhaps Daniel had been derelict in his duties earlier on,
but no one had caught the mistake. They searched to the point
of exhaustion, only to end their quest unsuccessfully. As much
as they hated to admit it, Daniel was apparently as good as
everyone said he was.

The only thing they could find wrong with him was that he
served God. What a marvelous indictment, and would it not be
wonderful if our detractors were to say the same thing about
you and me? But it will only be said about us as we remain
people of the Book who live on our knees in devoted worship
to our heavenly Father. It's what Luke says as he reminds us of

the words of Jesus, "And he spake a parable unto them to this end, that men ought always to pray, and not to faint" (Luke 18:1). That's our choice: We can either pray or faint. It's either one or the other, and Daniel never stopped praying. Because of this, his fellow administrators figured they'd finally discovered the smoking gun they were looking for, and that's when their treachery began. Today we might call it "bootlicking"—cozying up to someone from whom we might want a favor or some special arrangement. This is what Daniel's "friends" did by going to Darius with their newly-hatched scheme to catch Daniel in the act of praying. It's important to realize that it was not just a few who plotted against Daniel.

> *The vote was 122 to 1. How could any politician survive those odds? And it all started with a vile, dirty little sin called jealousy.*

Remember, there were 120 princes and three presidents—the first of whom was Daniel. That means there were 122 government servants under the Medes and the Persians who had turned against Daniel. The vote was 122 to 1. How could any politician survive those odds? And it all started with a vile, dirty little sin called jealousy. You might say, *Well, I don't go out and get drunk; I don't commit adultery; I don't steal; I have never murdered a person.* . . but if your heart is filled with envy, that not-so-small sin will remove you from the presence of God eternally unless repentance occurs. Galatians 5:19–21 reads, "Now the works of the flesh are manifest, which are these; Adultery, fornication, uncleanness, lasciviousness, idolatry,

witchcraft, hatred, variance, emulations, wrath, strife, sedi-
tions, heresies, Envyings, murders, drunkenness, revellings, and
such like: of the which I tell you before, as I have also told you
in time past, that they which do such things shall not inherit the
kingdom of God."

God's Word is constantly reminding us to check out our
hearts, and find out if we are envious of the position, wealth,
or appearance of others. Daniel didn't compare himself with
the Smiths and the Joneses of his day, and neither should we.
Daniel had higher goals, and his message to us is that if we are
to truly know God, we, too, must have goals and objectives
that reflect our love for the Savior. Meanwhile, Daniel's enemies got their way as they pushed through a decree that
promised a den filled with lions for those who worshipped any
god other than the king. What a fool-proof idea. Finally, they
would get this Jew who had been elevated to such a lofty position of leadership. Yes, a den of lions. That would surely do it.
Not even a praying Daniel could extricate himself from those
hungry beasts. Something else: They reminded the king that
when a decree is signed, it is an irrevocable law of the Medes
and the Persians. The king knew this, but because of the pressure of virtually his entire administrative staff, he complied
with their wishes, signing the document on the spot.

Daniel Caught in the Act—of Praying

10 *Now when Daniel knew that the writing was signed,*
he went into his house; and his windows being open
in his chamber toward Jerusalem, he kneeled upon his
knees three times a day, and prayed, and gave thanks
before his God, as he did aforetime.

11 *Then these men assembled, and found Daniel praying*
and making supplication before his God.

12 Then they came near, and spake before the king concerning the king's decree; Hast thou not signed a
decree, that every man that shall ask a petition of any
God or man within thirty days, save of thee, O king,
shall be cast into the den of lions? The king answered
and said, The thing is true, according to the law of the
Medes and Persians, which altereth not.

13 Then answered they and said before the king, That
Daniel, which is of the children of the captivity of
Judah, regardeth not thee, O king, nor the decree that
thou hast signed, but maketh his petition three times a
day.

14 Then the king, when he heard these words, was sore
displeased with himself, and set his heart on Daniel to
deliver him: and he laboured till the going down of
the sun to deliver him.

15 Then these men assembled unto the king, and said
unto the king, Know, O king, that the law of the
Medes and Persians is, That no decree nor statute
which the king establisheth may be changed.

> *He wanted everyone to know*
> *what he was doing and to*
> *whom he gave his allegiance as*
> *he bowed his head humbly*
> *toward Jerusalem, not toward*
> *the headquarters of the Medes*
> *and the Persians.*

These verses are a mini-treatise of what true friendship is all about, even though it may seem to be expressed in a context we might not expect. Here is a powerful king, Darius, who has signed a decree under considerable duress, now only to be made aware that his friend, counselor, and confidant, Daniel, has been "caught in the act" of praying to the God of the Hebrews. I've seen some Christians "scratch their eyebrows" as they bowed their heads and intoned a quick prayer in a restaurant, hoping that no one would see them praying before eating their food. Not Daniel. No secretive scratching of Jewish eyebrows for this saint of God.

Daniel knew the decree had been signed, and that his life was on the line. Yet, he continued to pray three times a day, as was the Jewish custom, and not just pray, but pray before an open window! He wanted everyone to know what he was doing and to whom he gave his allegiance as he bowed his head humbly toward Jerusalem, not toward the headquarters of the Medes and the Persians.

Matthew 10:32–33 reminds us that, "Whosoever therefore shall confess me before men, him will I confess also before my Father which is in heaven. But whosoever shall deny me before men, him will I also deny before my Father which is in heaven." It was true in Daniel's day, and it is true in ours. God doesn't put much stock in would-be believers who quietly "scratch their eyebrows" for fear of being caught in the act of praying.

Later, Jesus added, "Whosoever therefore shall be ashamed of me and of my words in this adulterous and sinful generation; of him also shall the Son of man be ashamed, when he cometh in the glory of his Father with the holy angels" (Mark 8:38). While the first six chapters of Daniel are more historical and devotional, do not forget that the essential content of Daniel—seen more graphically in the last six chapters—is about the return of Messiah, the coming again of Christ, a moment in time when Jesus will remind us that if we have been ashamed of Him, He will be ashamed of us. It cuts both ways.

The crown hangs forever heavy on the head of any ruler, and this night the head of Darius was heavy indeed. He realized he'd been tricked by his own staff just so they could get their man. The problem was that their man was also Darius's man—but for completely different reasons. Darius loved Daniel. It didn't matter that Daniel was a Jew in exile, that he was well up in years, or that he continued to worship the God of Father Abraham. Daniel was his friend, and Darius loved him. But now his friend was about to be thrown into a den of lions—and it was all his fault. Love—real love—seeks to overrule even the strictest, most binding decree. But, in this case, not even Darius's friendship with Daniel would be enough to save the day or the man. He had signed the proclamation. He had bowed to the pressure of putting himself in a position to be worshipped. Now, he would pay the consequence by losing his dear friend.

That evening, the kingly head tossed and turned, unable to sleep. Darius wished he could undo his terrible decree, but it was a law that could not be altered. An eighty-five-year-old saint and friend was about to be devoured by hungry lions, and that's all Darius could think about throughout the long, painful night.

Daniel's Punishment

16 *Then the king commanded, and they brought Daniel, and cast him into the den of lions. Now the king spake and said unto Daniel, Thy God whom thou servest continually, he will deliver thee.*

17 *And a stone was brought, and laid upon the mouth of the den; and the king sealed it with his own signet,*

and with the signet of his lords; that the purpose
might not be changed concerning Daniel.

18 *Then the king went to his palace, and passed the night*
fasting: neither were instruments of music brought
before him: and his sleep went from him.

> *Darius was rooting for his*
> *friend Daniel and was*
> *praying that his God*
> *would see him through the*
> *disastrous ordeal.*

Darius found himself between a rock and a hard place. He had to do the deed, and Daniel was brought to what all assumed would be his imminent death. But note what the king said in verse 16, "Thy God whom thou servest continually, he will deliver thee." What a vote of confidence for Daniel. Darius was rooting for his friend Daniel and was praying that his God would see him through the disastrous ordeal. But would it be enough to spare Daniel the pain and physical destruction of his body?

Many people have asked me, "Why did Darius use a lion's den when the fiery furnace was still in existence?" This is because the Babylonians—the former rulers—made it their practice to use a furnace as the primary vehicle to execute dissidents and enemies, as they'd attempted to do with the three Hebrew children. But now, under a new administration—the Medes and the Persians—this was not the appropriate means of execution. Here's the reason. The Medes and the Persians gave their allegiance to a religion called Zoroastrianism, and they worshipped the fire god, Atar. For them to use fire to execute their enemies would be to desecrate their teachings, putting them on the verge of religious sacrilege. Their alternative to fire was a large den of ravenously hungry lions, not the cage of sleepy beasts we might see lying about when we visit the lion section of a local zoo. This lion's den was an immense square cavern carved out of the ground to about the size of a large home. In the middle of the cavern was a partition with doors. From above, the workers could manipulate the doors to make them open and close. When they wanted to clean the den, they would jump down on the one side in safety because the lions were held back by the partition. When they wanted to throw raw meat—or their screaming enemies—to the hungry beasts, they would do just the opposite. Now, it was Daniel's turn to be lowered to the floor of the cavern below. The lions were hungry, pawing at the partition, ready to eat whatever would be placed on the other side of the door. We can only surmise what was in Daniel's mind as he waited for the panel to open.

With the stone on the den now firmly in place—sealed by the king and then again by his officials—the drama was ready to unfold. Apparently Darius did not choose to see what he feared might be the inevitable. Instead, he returned to his palace where he spent yet another sleepless night. The usual dancing girls, animated orchestra, rich foods, and night of revelry were canceled. Instead, Darius fasted—praying, in his own way, for the God of the Hebrews to put His cloak of protection around his friend.

"I'm OK, O King . . ."

19 Then the king arose very early in the morning, and went in haste unto the den of lions.

20 And when he came to the den, he cried with a lamentable voice unto Daniel: and the king spake and said

to Daniel, O Daniel, servant of the living God, is thy God, whom thou servest continually, able to deliver thee from the lions?

21 *Then said Daniel unto the king, O king, live for ever.*

22 *My God hath sent his angel, and hath shut the lions' mouths, that they have not hurt me: forasmuch as before him innocency was found in me; and also before thee, O king, have I done no hurt.*

23 *Then was the king exceeding glad for him, and commanded that they should take Daniel up out of the den. So Daniel was taken up out of the den, and no manner of hurt was found upon him, because he believed in his God.*

> *The time between the king's cry and Daniel's response must have seemed like an eternity to Darius. Then, the king heard what he wanted to hear.*

Perhaps you've had a loved one who was sent to the hospital emergency ward. You prayed all night for his or her recovery. But you've received no word. All night you wondered, worried, and prayed for the one you loved. Then, early the next morning, you jumped into your car and rushed to the hospital to check on the person for whom you cared so much. Well, that's how Darius must have felt when he rose from his bed at the breaking of dawn the next morning. He didn't stay around for his usual bath or breakfast, or to be waited on by his servants. He had only one objective: to go to the lion's den and check on the condition of his friend. I can almost feel his heavy breathing as he made the trek from his sleeping chamber to the large cavern where the lions were kept. Would Daniel be alive? Or would there only be a few scraps of bones?

When he arrived at the den, his voice cracked and trembled as he cried out, "Daniel, O Daniel, servant of the living God, is thy God, whom thou servest continually, able to deliver thee from the lions?" The time between the king's cry and Daniel's response must have seemed like an eternity to Darius. Then, the king heard what he wanted to hear—what any friend wants to hear about a friend in trouble—that he was all right. The score was:

Daniel—1

Lions—0

It's no accident that the writer of the Book of Hebrews would later write about this victorious deliverance when he stated: "Who through faith subdued kingdoms, wrought righteousness, obtained promises, stopped the mouths of lions" (Hebrews 11:33). God had indeed paralyzed the mouths of what may have been as many as two hundred hungry lions, and Daniel's life was spared. Picture the scene: A king and his friend are reunited, as Daniel is pulled back up through the opening in the cavern. The prayers of both men were heard as God again venerated Daniel's loyalty, faith, and allegiance.

Keep the Lions Handy—and Hungry

24 And the king commanded, and they brought those
men which had accused Daniel, and they cast them

into the den of lions, them, their children, and their
wives; and the lions had the mastery of them, and
brake all their bones in pieces or ever they came at the
bottom of the den.

The wheels of justice moved swiftly that day as the king commanded that all 120 princes, two presidents, and their families be rounded up and brought to the cavern. The law of the Medes and Persians stated that whatever punishment was meted out to a leader, his family would also experience. So if we consider an average family of the day to be four persons, there could have been as many as five hundred individuals dropped through the ceiling into the lion's den, where the beasts—thwarted from having a good meal the night before—ripped their prey to shreds. Some, in fact, were killed mid-air, since the verse says, "the lions had the mastery of them, and brake all their bones in pieces or ever they came at the bottom of the den" (6:24). No more would Darius be subjected to their jealousy and rage. The punishment they'd designed for Daniel was now their own undoing. By also killing his leaders' families, the king had eliminated the possibility of reprisals, and even potential assassination attempts on himself.

These were not toothless lions as some have suggested. They were the same beasts that had simply skipped a meal to be used to destroy the jealousy-filled conspirators against God's prophet. The message of this passage? Be careful not to attack the prophets of God—God's duly ordained ministers. Psalm 105:15 says, "Touch not mine anointed, and do my prophets no harm." It is your duty and mine to obey God, and to give honor and respect to those who declare the word of truth. Some of today's "lions" waiting to devour God's servants may not be of the four-legged variety, but they, too, will surely pay

the price if they demonstrate by their actions that they are fail-
ing to live in obedience to God's warning about His servants.

A New Proclamation Is Issued

25 *Then king Darius wrote unto all people, nations, and
languages, that dwell in all the earth; Peace be multiplied unto you.*

26 *I make a decree, That in every dominion of my kingdom men tremble and fear before the God of Daniel:
for he is the living God, and stedfast for ever, and his
kingdom that which shall not be destroyed, and his
dominion shall be even unto the end.*

27 *He delivereth and rescueth, and he worketh signs and
wonders in heaven and in earth, who hath delivered
Daniel from the power of the lions.*

28 *So this Daniel prospered in the reign of Darius, and in
the reign of Cyrus the Persian.*

*Have you ever been there?
Where all your best laid
plans, investments, manipulation of people and events
have simply not given you
what you really wanted
from life?*

Zoroaster and Atar, the god of fire, could not do the job. The
lions couldn't do what the enemy had set them up to do.

Treachery born of avarice had not won the day. It was the living God who again stepped in and reminded the Gentile establishment that enough was enough. I've always wondered why Darius did not fall on his knees and get converted right there on the spot. Perhaps he did, and we just do not have the written account. But I have a sneaking suspicion that as he made his decree for all his subjects to serve Daniel's God, in his heart he may have said, "My beloved Daniel, I want your God. I want a God in my life who can paralyze the mouths of two hundred hungry lions. I want a God to do what Zoroaster and Atar cannot do. I want a God who is faithful and true, and not subject to human whim."

Have you ever been there? Where all your best laid plans, investments, manipulation of people and events have simply not given you what you really wanted from life? I'm sure we've all had those experiences. That's why we must remember that there comes a time when only the Holy Spirit can do the job. Jesus said, in John 6:44, "No man can come to me, except the Father which hath sent me draw him." This is one of the key messages of this chapter. You see, this is more than simply a story about Daniel in a den of hungry lions. It's a narrative of God's enormous power, great love, compassionate mercy, overwhelming friendship, and the timeless reality that He will always have the last word in every situation—lions present or not. These first six chapters are prologue to the great prophecies yet to come—simply reminders that earthly kingdoms will always come and go, but the kingdom of God is an eternal one, the warm-up message for what we will now begin to analyze in chapters seven through twelve, the prophetic portion of the Book of Daniel.

❧·Part II·❧

Events Prophesied . . .
Prophecies Fulfilled

❧ 7 ❧

Beasts, Beasts, and More Beasts

Note to the reader: As we prepare our hearts to hear the message of God in Daniel chapters seven through twelve, it's important to remember that Daniel often spoke of visions and dreams that he encountered later in his life. Some he received prior to the events of chapters five and six; at least one was received later.

DANIEL 7:1–14

1 *In the first year of Belshazzar king of Babylon Daniel had a dream and visions of his head upon his bed: then he wrote the dream, and told the sum of the matters.*

2 *Daniel spake and said, I saw in my vision by night, and, behold, the four winds of the heaven strove upon the great sea.*

3 *And four great beasts came up from the sea, diverse one from another.*

4 *The first was like a lion, and had eagle's wings: I beheld till the wings thereof were plucked, and it was lifted up from the earth, and made stand upon the feet as a man, and a man's heart was given to it.*

5 *And behold another beast, a second, like to a bear,*
  and it raised up itself on one side, and it had three
  ribs in the mouth of it between the teeth of it: and
  they said thus unto it, Arise, devour much flesh.

6 *After this I beheld, and lo another, like a leopard,*
  which had upon the back of it four wings of a fowl;
  the beast had also four heads; and dominion was
  given to it.

7 *After this I saw in the night visions, and behold a*
  fourth beast, dreadful and terrible, and strong exceed-
  ingly; and it had great iron teeth: it devoured and
  brake in pieces, and stamped the residue with the feet
  of it: and it was diverse from all the beasts that were
  before it; and it had ten horns.

8 *I considered the horns, and, behold, there came up*
  among them another little horn, before whom there
  were three of the first horns plucked up by the roots:
  and, behold, in this horn were eyes like the eyes of
  man, and a mouth speaking great things.

9 *I beheld till the thrones were cast down, and the*
  Ancient of days did sit, whose garment was white as
  snow, and the hair of his head like the pure wool: his
  throne was like the fiery flame, and his wheels as
  burning fire.

10 *A fiery stream issued and came forth from before him:*
   thousand thousands ministered unto him, and ten
   thousand times ten thousand stood before him: the
   judgment was set, and the books were opened.

11 *I beheld then because of the voice of the great words which the horn spake: I beheld even till the beast was slain, and his body destroyed, and given to the burning flame.*

12 *As concerning the rest of the beasts, they had their dominion taken away: yet their lives were prolonged for a season and time.*

13 *I saw in the night visions, and, behold, one like the Son of man came with the clouds of heaven, and came to the Ancient of days, and they brought him near before him.*

14 *And there was given him dominion, and glory, and a kingdom, that all people, nations, and languages, should serve him: his dominion is an everlasting dominion, which shall not pass away, and his kingdom that which shall not be destroyed.*

WE ARE NOW GOING to move away from the historical material that we encountered in chapters one through six and plunge into the exciting depths of Daniel's prophetic material, starting in chapter seven. Daniel's end-time dream in this chapter consisted of symbols of real events to come—mysteries we are now able to unravel. In many ways, chapters two and seven of the Book of Daniel are similar in that they portray the most comprehensive pictures of history to its conclusion. Chapter two depicted Nebuchadnezzar's dream concerning the great statue with a head of gold down to its feet and toes of iron mixed with clay—a prediction of how the

Babylonian empire would be destroyed by Medo-Persia, followed by the conquering superpowers of Greece and Rome. Chapter seven refers to these identical empires in the form of beasts, indicating that within the final revived Roman Empire there will be many problems during the course of its restoration. In fact, one major challenge after another can already be observed within the framework of the European Union presently taking shape. To the extent we saw unity in chapter two, we see diversity in chapter seven. But regardless of the message, the single most exciting thing that you are now reading is the fulfillment of Daniel 12:4, which says, "But thou, O Daniel, shut up the words, and seal the book, even to the time of the end: many shall run to and fro, and knowledge shall be increased." The Book of Daniel was designed to be a mysterious, closed, sealed book until the time of the end, but at the time of the end the Holy Spirit would enlighten people to expound this great portion of God's Word. This is now our assignment, and you are privileged to have a ringside seat as we begin to unravel the mysteries so long alien to anyone's understanding.

> *Isn't it fascinating that from*
> *June 5 through June 10, 1967—*
> *as a result of the Six-Day War—*
> *the Jews took back Jerusalem*
> *and have been in control of the*
> *Holy City ever since?*

The Times of the Gentiles

The Jewish people controlled Jerusalem until 586 B.C. Then, according to Daniel 1:1, Nebuchadnezzar and his troops marched into the Holy City and took its inhabitants back as captives to Babylon. It is important to remember that this single historical event marked the beginning of what is known as "the times of the Gentiles." An important caveat was spoken by Jesus in Luke 21:24 when He said, "And they shall fall by the edge of the sword, and shall be led away captive into all nations: and Jerusalem shall be trodden down of the Gentiles, until the times of the Gentiles be fulfilled." Jesus was saying that Jerusalem would remain under Gentile control until the time of the end. Isn't it fascinating that from June 5 through June 10, 1967—as a result of the Six-Day War—the Jews took back Jerusalem and have been in control of the Holy City ever since? Even though we are still in the era called "the times of the Gentiles," this remarkable historical reality reminds us how close we are to the time of the end. How can we say this with such certainty? In Zechariah 14:2–4 God states:

> For I will gather all nations against Jerusalem to battle; and the city shall be taken, and the houses rifled, and the women ravished; and half of the city shall go forth into captivity, and the residue of the people shall not be cut off from the city. Then shall the LORD go forth, and fight against those nations, as when he fought in the day of battle. And his feet shall stand in that day upon the mount of Olives, which is before Jerusalem on the east, and the mount of Olives shall cleave in the midst thereof toward the east and toward the west, and there shall be a very great valley; and half of the mountain shall remove toward the north, and half of it toward the south.

This entire scenario began with Nebuchadnezzar in 586 B.C. and ends when Jesus Christ returns to take Jerusalem back from the Gentiles. We are extremely close to that time when such an event takes place. Here's why. The Gentiles could not take Jerusalem from the Jews until the Jews controlled the city—which happened in 1967 after 2,553 years of Gentile dominion. According to Jesus, the generation who lives to see this event will be alive for the battle to recapture Jerusalem by the Gentiles plus observe Christ's return.

The Four Beasts

Daniel dreams about four winds and four beasts—all which represent the same four powers we read about in Nebuchadnezzar's dream in chapter two: Babylon, Medo-Persia, Greece, and Rome, along with the ten toes of iron mixed with clay—a description of the revived Roman Empire, a regrouping of nations I believe to be the European Union. The fourth beast has ten horns, similar to the ten toes on Nebuchadnezzar's image: again, symbolic of the restored Roman Empire. The four winds blowing upon the sea indicate trouble—and all these nations near the Sea of Galilee, the Dead Sea, and the Mediterranean have indeed experienced troublesome times throughout history. However, only when the European Union ultimately produces the Antichrist will the world truly know what real trouble is. It will be nothing like the nuisance these nations have been prior to this time in history. Isaiah 57:20 states, "But the wicked are like the troubled sea, when it cannot rest, whose waters cast up mire and dirt."

Now let's look at the four beasts and indicate what each represents. Beast number one—a lion with the wings of eagles—is the same power that was described in Nebuchadnezzar's dream as the "head of gold"—the Babylonian empire. The wings of the lion suggest that it is a swift beast, with the ability to conquer great nations with its mighty armies. But as its wings are "plucked," the kingdom begins to deteriorate, even though there remains a hint of Nebuchadnezzar's humanitarianism. Since verse 4 makes reference to this first beast "being given a man's heart," you'll recall that this is the manner in which Nebuchadnezzar closed out his days after his conversion experience—compassionate, docile, and caring for his subjects.

Beast number two is a bear that raises itself up on one side, holding three ribs in its teeth—conceivably representing Lydia, Babylon, and Egypt—a hungry beast, and capable of gorging itself. Following the pattern of Nebuchadnezzar's image, this second beast is a symbol of the Medes and the Persians, with Darius ruler of the Medes and Cyrus the Persians. Ultimately, however, the Persians demonstrated greater strength because of their massive armies, and, as a result, the bear "lifted itself up on one side," indicating Persian political and military superiority, all borne out by historical fact.

Beast number three is Greece, a leopard with four wings and four heads. The wings picture the speed of Alexander the Great and his enormous armies, reckoned to be the swiftest in the known world. Alexander conquered one and one-half million square miles of the globe, stretching for more than eleven thousand miles from Greece in the west to India in the east, a man who, even after his many conquests, is said to have wept because he felt he had no more worlds to conquer.

Beast number four is Rome—a terrible beast with enormous power to maim, crush, and kill. So violent is this beast that no animal on earth can represent it. Its iron teeth are similar to the toes on the image composed of iron mixed with clay as observed in Daniel chapter two. Its ten horns are a graphic description of the final revived Roman Empire—fulfilled in 1981 when Greece became the tenth nation to join the European Union.

> *Dr. Harry Ironside, pastor of*
> *Moody Memorial Church, said*
> *there will arise a great confed-*
> *eracy of nations springing*
> *forth from an old Roman*
> *Empire that will become the*
> *devil's last trump card.*

Some people ask me, How can these things be? How can you be so certain that your interpretation of Daniel's dream is correct? First of all, the nations are mentioned by name in Daniel 1:1, 8:20, 8:21, and Romans 1:7. These empires cover a period of 676 years. Adding scholarship to the truth of God's Word, a prophet by the name of Esdras wrote in 90 A.D. that there was little doubt that the fourth beast was Rome. Add to these the research insights of Drs. Gabelein, Scofield, Bultima, Ironside, Barnhouse, DeHaan and other evangelical scholars, and the evidence mounts that the only possible meaning of the symbolic fourth beast is Rome itself. Specifically, Dr. Harry Ironside, pastor of Moody Memorial Church, said there will arise a great confederacy of nations springing forth from an old Roman Empire that will become the devil's last trump card.

The Plot Thickens . . . and Will Get Thicker

Yet, it is only within the last century that God has been unsealing the mysteries of this book and Daniel's dream. While the significance of the first three beasts is relatively easy to interpret because of its solid basis in historical fact, the ten toes (Daniel 2:41–42, 44) and the ten horns (Daniel 7:7, 20, 24 and Revelation 12:3; 13:1; 17:3, 7, 12, 16) must now be addressed in some detail. To do this, we need to go back to the year 1947 when Benelux came into power: Belgium, the Netherlands, and Luxembourg—the first three horns on the terrible fourth beast, and the first three nations of what presently comprises the European Union. In 1957, France, Italy, and Germany joined the confederation, making it six, with the Treaty of Rome ratifying this amalgamation. In 1973, Britain, Ireland, and Denmark joined for a total of nine. Then, on January 1, 1981, Greece joined the group to make it ten in number. At this point many evangelicals were elated, making the assumption that all the members of the group had finally been assembled. However, in Daniel 7:8, 20, and 24 we read that the confederation will grow to thirteen. This has already taken place: Numbers eleven and twelve who joined the EU were Spain and Portugal, coming into the confederation in 1986. Then with the arrival of Austria into the movement in 1996, the EU grew to thirteen.

But this is only the beginning. Eventually the fourth beast becomes a world empire—the New World Order, something we are already beginning to witness. Daniel 7:23 states that he shall devour (or engulf) the whole world. Revelation 13:7 adds: "Power was given him over all kindreds, and tongues, and nations." No longer is this fulfillment of prophecy something you and I read about in the Book of Daniel alone, but it is also the subject matter for the correspondents and editors of the pages of your daily newspaper: Prophecy is being fulfilled in black and white each day for those who have eyes to see and ears to hear.

The Little Horn

Now let's look at the "little horn" of Daniel 7:8. Who and what is it? What is its influence? Martin Luther said that this little horn is the New Testament Antichrist of the future, and I agree. This little horn's appearance was not for an earlier period in history, but for the end time of Daniel 12:4. Why? Because this little horn—the Antichrist—arises at the last day out of this grouping of ten nations. Since the European Union is now in place, there is little question that the Antichrist can—and will—arise soon.

> *The Antichrist blasphemes God almighty and eventually calls himself God, but at a great cost to this "beast". . .*

The Beast Speaks

Verse 11 says the little horn, or beast, speaks, and his words are great. This event takes place during the Tribulation hour, when the little horn, the infamous Antichrist, finally arises and comes to power. Revelation 13:5 and 6 add, "And there was given unto him a mouth speaking great things and blasphemies; and power was given unto him to continue forty and two months. And he opened his mouth in blasphemy against God, to blaspheme his name, and his tabernacle, and them that dwell in heaven." The Antichrist blasphemes God almighty and eventually calls himself God, but at a great cost to this "beast" because Jesus Christ will destroy him with the brightness of His coming (2 Thessalonians 2:8). However, there is even more devastation ahead as the beast and the false prophet are cast into the lake of fire burning with fire and brimstone (Revelation 19:20). Furthermore, when Satan is cast into the lake of fire one thousand years later, the beast and the false prophet are still in existence—proving that the fires of hell do not annihilate anyone, as some cults teach (Revelation 20:10).

And what about the other beasts in Daniel's dream? When do they have their dominion taken from them? This is a fascinating question, and an important one. The Medes and the Persians destroyed Babylon; Greece destroyed the Medes and the Persians, and Rome destroyed Greece. Their kingdoms and powers were taken away. Yet, the passage tells us that they still exist because all their customs and cultures were passed on to each nation that conquered them, meaning they are all still with us in some way. Remember that the old Persian Empire is today's Iran and Iraq. Would you not agree these two nations are still with us, continuing to create havoc in the area and around the world with their commitment to regional conflict and international terrorism?

The Son of Man and the Ancient of Days

In his dream, Daniel had a vision of one like the Son of Man coming with the clouds of heaven. This is none other than the Lord Jesus Christ. This prophecy is about to happen because the term *Son of Man* is definitely the Messiah and the Savior. Let's investigate further. The term *Son of Man* is the precise one Jesus used repeatedly to describe Himself. Matthew 8:20 says, "And Jesus saith unto him, The foxes have holes, and the birds of the air have nests; but the Son of man hath not where to lay his head." Matthew 24:30 tells us, "And then shall appear the sign of the Son of man in heaven: and then shall all the tribes of the earth mourn, and they shall see the Son of man coming in the clouds of heaven with power and great glory."

Now the Ancient of Days—*Yahweh*—presents the kingdom to His Son, Jesus Christ. This is the moment when the stone cut out without hands smashes the feet of the image in Daniel 2:45. This announces the return of Christ because He is the stone or rock (1 Corinthians 10:4). Then comes the tremendous battle we read about in Revelation 19 when Christ comes on a white horse (v. 11) and the armies of heaven follow Him (v. 14). Verse 19 says, "And I saw the beast [the Antichrist, the little horn], and the kings of the earth, and their armies, gathered together to make war against him [Jesus] that sat on the horse, and against his army." But they do not prevail. This is the time when the prophecy of the stone smashing the feet of the image is fulfilled. It's all over for the world powers at this point because Jesus Christ has arrived to set up His Kingdom. However, as the Lord appears, the armies of the revived Roman Empire attempt to stop the King of Kings and Lord of Lords (Revelation 19:19–21). Psalm 2:1–6 pictures this final battle:

> Why do the heathen rage, and the people imagine a vain thing? The kings of the earth set themselves, and the rulers take counsel together, against the LORD, and against his anointed, saying, Let us break their bands asunder, and cast away their cords from us. He that sitteth in the heavens shall laugh: the LORD shall have them in derision. Then shall he speak unto them in his wrath, and vex them in his sore displeasure. Yet have I set my king upon my holy hill of Zion.

This will be the great climax, that moment in history when Gentile dominion ends, and when Jesus Christ is seated on the throne of David. Luke 1:32–33 says, "He shall be great, and shall be called the Son of the Highest: and the Lord God shall give unto him the throne of his father David: And he shall reign over the house of Jacob for ever; and of his kingdom there shall be no end." After the thousand-year reign of Christ, the earth is purged and Christ is recommissioned and rules eternally upon earth (1 Corinthians 15:24–28). That's why Ephesians 3:21

adds, "Unto Him be glory in the church by Christ Jesus throughout all ages, world without end. Amen."

Daniel's Response

15 *I Daniel was grieved in my spirit in the midst of my body, and the visions of my head troubled me.*

16 *I came near unto one of them that stood by, and asked him the truth of all this. So he told me, and made me know the interpretation of the things.*

17 *These great beasts, which are four, are four kings, which shall arise out of the earth.*

18 *But the saints of the most High shall take the kingdom, and possess the kingdom for ever, even for ever and ever.*

19 *Then I would know the truth of the fourth beast, which was diverse from all the others, exceeding dreadful, whose teeth were of iron, and his nails of brass; which devoured, brake in pieces, and stamped the residue with his feet;*

20 *And of the ten horns that were in his head, and of the other which came up, and before whom three fell; even of that horn that had eyes, and a mouth that spake very great things, whose look was more stout than his fellows.*

21 *I beheld, and the same horn made war with the saints, and prevailed against them;*

22 *Until the Ancient of days came, and judgment was given to the saints of the most High; and the time came that the saints possessed the kingdom.*

23 *Thus he said, The fourth beast shall be the fourth kingdom upon earth, which shall be diverse from all kingdoms, and shall devour the whole earth, and shall tread it down, and break it in pieces.*

24 *And the ten horns out of this kingdom are ten kings that shall arise: and another shall rise after them; and he shall be diverse from the first, and he shall subdue three kings.*

25 *And he shall speak great words against the most High, and shall wear out the saints of the most High, and think to change times and laws: and they shall be given into his hand until a time and times and the dividing of time.*

26 *But the judgment shall sit, and they shall take away his dominion, to consume and to destroy it unto the end.*

27 *And the kingdom and dominion, and the greatness of the kingdom under the whole heaven, shall be given to the people of the saints of the most High, whose kingdom is an everlasting kingdom, and all dominions shall serve and obey him.*

Daniel Is Confused

Daniel had no one to help him understand what he had been dreaming, so God provided a messenger to interpret the dream on His behalf—the angel Gabriel. The message of chapter two, Nebuchadnezzar's dream, had been so clear and unified, whereas now his own dream was filled with diversity, the edges of his understanding ragged, all because he was dealing with four terrible, vile beasts—not an immense one-piece image of gold, silver, and bronze—but a diversity of four beasts acting out their beastly nature in fits of anger, violence, and conquest. Then, suddenly, something exciting happens in verse 18 where the saints of the most High take the Kingdom. This is when Jesus Christ returns, and, as we have already stated, the stone smites the feet of the image, placing Christ and His saints in control. They are the ones who return with Jesus—individuals who missed the terrible seven-year period of Tribulation because they were called up in Revelation 4:1.

In Revelation 19:11–14, when Christ returns on that white horse, we discover that the armies in heaven follow Him—a picture of the Church returning to earth. Jude verse 14b says, "Behold, the Lord cometh with ten thousands of his saints." They had no way of saying millions, billions, or trillions in the first century, so they used the term *tens of thousands*. But there is also the group of saints—the 144,000 Jewish messengers (Revelation 7:4–8)—who preached the gospel of the Kingdom (Matthew 24:14). You see, not only will many Jews be converted through mass, worldwide efforts of evangelism, but multitudes—yes, millions—of Gentiles will also be saved, many of whom are put to death for loving the Word of God. Revelation 20:4–5 speaks of this treachery:

And I saw thrones, and they sat upon them, and judgment was given unto them: and I saw the souls of them that were beheaded for the witness of Jesus, and for the word of God, and which had not worshipped the beast, neither his image, neither had received his mark upon their foreheads, or in their hands; and they lived and reigned with Christ a thousand years. But the rest of the dead lived not again until the thousand years were finished. This is the first resurrection.

The saints are coming from heaven. Those who have died

during the tribulation are then raised from the dead (Revelation 20:4). The Jews in Daniel 12:2 who "slept in the dust of the earth" also awaken, while Gentiles who died for their testimony also arise. Now we have saints from heaven, tribulation saints who were brought back from the dead, Jewish saints who also were resurrected, and saints who are still alive on earth at Christ's return who somehow escaped the death penalty for rejecting the "mark of the beast" (Matthew 25:31–46; Revelation 13:15–18). They will all rule and reign with Jesus Christ, giving further credence to the passage, "If we suffer, we shall also reign with him" (2 Timothy 2:12a).

> *Rome—and a revived Roman Empire—would come centuries later, and he could have known nothing about it.*

The European Community—Antichrist—and 666

While general concern may have reigned in Daniel's mind regarding much of the dream, there seemed to be a special confusion regarding the fourth beast. Daniel had a reasonably adequate understanding of Babylon, the Medes and the Persians, and Greece, largely since they already existed within his own time frame. But this next beast—Rome—and the revived Roman Empire—would come centuries later, and he could not, in his day, know anything about this mystery without the enlightenment of the Holy Spirit concerning end-time events. This was the empire with the two legs and ten toes, and the animal with ten horns that was a composite of all the others. Ten toes and ten horns. Try though he might, Daniel could not grasp their meaning. Yet now, twenty-five hundred years later, you and I are on the edge of watching such mysteries unfold as the European Union flexes its international muscles, preparing the world community for the advent of the Antichrist. During the terrible Tribulation hour, the Jewish people are primarily the saints against whom the Antichrist prevails. Jeremiah 30:7 says, "Alas! for that day is great, so that none is like it: it is even the time of Jacob's trouble."

Jacob is another name for Israel (2 Kings 17:34). We find that when Satan is cast to earth he becomes extremely angry when he realizes his time is exceedingly short (Revelation 12:12). For this reason, he makes every attempt to obliterate the Jewish race (Revelation 12:13). He persecutes the woman who brought forth the manchild—that woman is the Jewish virgin, Mary. The Son that came from her is that manchild, and this Antichrist is trying to get rid of all those who came forth from her, as well as millions of Gentiles. Both groups find salvation during the Tribulation hour (Revelation 7:14). These are the ones who have come out of the Great Tribulation and have washed their robes, and made them white in the blood of the lamb.

At this point of time the Antichrist will call himself God, and the false prophet sets up an image of him to worship. The Bible says in Revelation 13:15, "And he had power to give life unto the image of the beast, that the image of the beast should both speak, and cause that as many as would not worship the image of the beast should be killed." He says, "Bow down and worship this image of me and take my mark '666' or you will lose your head" (see Revelation 13:15–18; 20:4). This is that period of time when the Antichrist will prevail over the saints. But to reiterate the good news, the Lord Jesus Christ ultimately returns as King of Kings and Lord of Lords (Revelation 19:16) and defeats the Antichrist and his hoards (Revelation 19:19–21; Psalm 2:1–6).

Good news indeed! At that crucial moment in history,

almighty God says, "How dare you think you can stand against me and my Son as I present Him to the world as King of Kings and Lord of Lords. You lose . . . because I now set up my King upon the holy hill of Jerusalem!"

The Reign of the Antichrist

Before we close this chapter, it's important to review the activity of the Antichrist for the eighty-four months that he appears on earth. His reign begins when he makes a peace contract with Israel and the nations. Daniel 9:27 says, "And he shall confirm the covenant with many for one week: and in the midst of the week he shall cause the sacrifice and the oblation to cease." The Hebrew word for *week* in the above passage is *shabua*, a time period of seven years, or eighty-four months. In the midst of the week or *shabua*—after forty-two months—he shall cause the sacrifice and the oblation to cease. His first item of business is to make peace with Israel, an agreement he honors for three and one-half years. At that point, however, Russia begins its march southward to Israel to break the peace contract that the Antichrist originally made with Israel. Then Gog and Magog (Russia) go up against the land of unwalled villages when Israel is at rest (Ezekiel 38:11).

We know that since she became a nation in 1948, Israel has neither been at rest nor at peace. Soon a peace program of seven years duration will be contracted. But it will be short-lived. Russia ruins it. During this battle the Antichrist comes to his end (Daniel 11:45). Yes, he actually dies, but Revelation 13:3 says, "his deadly wound was healed: and all the world wondered [marveled] after the beast." In other words, the Antichrist is resurrected. He comes back to life. That's why everyone marvels at him, literally standing in awe of his great political prowess and enormous ability to move the minds and hearts of people globally. To the world, he appears to be like

Jesus, returning to life. It's at this point he magnifies himself above every God (Daniel 11:36) and exalts himself above all gods to a deluded and deceived world (2 Thessalonians 2:4). He literally says, "I am God." Today, as you watch an acceleration of the New Age movement and its "I am God" philosophy, crystals, shamans, chants, and channeled messages that permeate every segment of our society—even entering the church of Jesus Christ—be aware that this global satanic activity has already proved instrumental in preparing the way for this great deceiver to set himself up for worship (Revelation 13:15), a time when he literally "wears out the saints" (Daniel 7:25). This activity takes place through to the end of the seven years when Jesus Christ ultimately returns and destroys the evil one with the brightness of His glory, casting him into the lake of fire where he remains forever and ever (Revelation 19:20).

Daniel's Reaction

28 *Hitherto is the end of the matter. As for me Daniel, my cogitations much troubled me, and my countenance changed in me: but I kept the matter in my heart.*

When his dream had been explained by the angel Gabriel, Daniel felt a sorrow of heart, for he now began to understand what would one day happen to his people, the Jews. His dream had helped him catch a glimpse of the terrible times of persecution that would fall upon them. He was rightly disturbed and confused because he was not totally privy to understanding the great blessings—the rest of the story—that would ultimately come to his people—blessings we will discover as we continue to unwrap the sealed mysteries of the time of the end, even as we see Daniel's humanity surface when he is physically and psychologically devastated by the vision he sees in chapter eight.

⁍·8·⁌

A Tale of Two Madmen

W E HAVE COME to the close of the section that addresses God's rule over the Gentiles. To help you understand where Daniel is emotionally at this point in
the book, I'd like you to put yourself in his position for a
moment. You have just dreamed something tantamount to a
nightmare in chapter seven that has unnerved you. You fainted,
you became anxious—so fearful that you needed help to interpret what you experienced. Now, you are taking your agitation
and dismay to the next practical level by asking yourself: *If
three more Gentile kingdoms, as suggested by the dream, are
supposed to arrive on the scene to dominate the world after
Babylon, what will be the fate of my people, the Jews, during
that period of time? How long will their trials last? What will
be the end result?* These vexing questions are coursing through
Daniel's mind, but still, he has no answers.

But God never leaves His people in a state of confusion. For
that reason, God begins to provide Daniel with specific revelations that relate to the future history of His people. With that
brief background, we now spend the remainder of the book
reviewing these revelations, giving special emphasis to interpreting the prophecies that address "the time of the end"—predictions that not only relate to Israel during the latter days, but
also speak to you and me—Jew or Gentile—today.

DANIEL 8:1–2

1 *In the third year of the reign of king Belshazzar a vision appeared unto me, even unto me Daniel, after that which appeared unto me at the first.*

2 *And I saw in a vision; and it came to pass, when I saw, that I was at Shushan in the palace, which is in the province of Elam; and I saw in a vision, and I was by the river of Ulai.*

The year is 551 B.C. Daniel sees himself at the Palace of Shushan, a city in Persia about 230 miles east of Babylon and 120 miles north of the Persian Gulf. Daniel makes it clear that this vision took place before his troubling dream in chapter seven. What we are about to learn is that the vision Daniel now sees again projects him into the future when the superpower Medo-Persia would rule the then-known world—a partial rerun of what Daniel has already learned in earlier dreams.

3 *Then I lifted up mine eyes, and saw, and, behold, there stood before the river a ram which had two horns: and the two horns were high; but one was higher than the other, and the higher came up last.*

4 *I saw the ram pushing westward, and northward, and southward; so that no beasts might stand before him, neither was there any that could deliver out of his hand; but he did according to his will, and became great.*

5 *And as I was considering, behold, an he goat came from the west on the face of the whole earth, and touched not the ground: and the goat had a notable horn between his eyes.*

6 *And he came to the ram that had two horns, which I had seen standing before the river, and ran unto him in the fury of his power.*

7 *And I saw him come close unto the ram, and he was moved with choler against him, and smote the ram, and brake his two horns: and there was no power in the ram to stand before him, but he cast him down to the ground, and stamped upon him: and there was none that could deliver the ram out of his hand.*

8 *Therefore the he goat waxed very great: and when he was strong, the great horn was broken; and for it came up four notable ones toward the four winds of heaven.*

9 *And out of one of them came forth a little horn, which waxed exceeding great, toward the south, and toward the east, and toward the pleasant land.*

10 *And it waxed great, even to the host of heaven; and it cast down some of the host and of the stars to the ground, and stamped upon them.*

11 *Yea, he magnified himself even to the prince of the host, and by him the daily sacrifice was taken away, and the place of his sanctuary was cast down.*

12 *And an host was given him against the daily sacrifice by reason of transgression, and it cast down the truth to the ground; and it practised, and prospered.*

13 *Then I heard one saint speaking, and another saint said unto that certain saint which spake, How long shall be the vision concerning the daily sacrifice, and the transgression of desolation, to give both the sanctuary and the host to be trodden under foot?*

14 *And he said unto me, Unto two thousand and three hundred days; then shall the sanctuary be cleansed.*

> *Now the ram goes into action, lowering its fierce head and butting at prey to the west, north, and south.*

New Symbolism—Same Message

Daniel's been here before. The difference is that in this vision the symbols have been changed. Just as the bear appeared in chapter seven as rising higher on one side, so, in similar fashion, there is now a picture of one of the horns of the ram rising higher than the other, indicating again the dominance the Persians exercised over their partners, the Medes. So far, this is not new information, but this reiteration does not diminish the significance of the drama.

The ram with the two horns standing before the Ulai River again represents Medo-Persia and corresponds to the arms and breast of silver we saw in chapter two and to the appearance of the bear in chapter seven. Historically, this is 100 percent correct, as we would expect. It's God's Word. We know that the symbolic, protective force of the Medes and the Persians was a ram with a sharp horn. Not only that, but the Persian ruler, when engaging in foreign military expeditions, proudly wore the head of a ram on his head as a symbol of his enormous power.

Now the ram goes into action, lowering its fierce head and butting at prey to the west, north, and south. Ultimately, as our history books tell us, Medo-Persia laid waste Babylonia, Asia

Minor, and Syria to the west; Armenia, and the area of the Caspian Sea to the north; and then conquered Ethiopia and Egypt to the south. Symbolized by a ram, the Medo-Persian empire butted up against virtually every nation and principality in sight and soon became the greatest power on the face of the earth. So far, this is more of a confirmation of Daniel's earlier dream than anything else, and such confirmation continues as we now see the nation of Greece symbolized by a goat, the equivalent of the brass stomach and thighs of Nebuchadnezzar's image in chapter two, and the leopard with wings in chapter seven. So fleet of foot is this goat that when it runs its feet do not touch the ground—an apt description of the awesome power of the swift, far-reaching campaigns of the Greco-Macedonian army.

Suddenly, however, the vision provides us with additional, detailed information, more than we saw in Daniel's earlier dream. Greece is not only the goat, but now we see a great horn appear between its eyes, a symbol of Greece's first great monarch, Alexander the Great. There had not been a military strategist the likes of Alexander in the annals of history. Son of the great militarist Philip of Macedon and student of Aristotle, Alexander, in the course of his short life, conquered one and one half million square miles. While in power, he was revered by all as a young king with singular skills and enormous intelligence, amazing the world with his military prowess. His crowning victory came with the destruction of the once-invincible Medo-Persian empire in less than a three-year interval— 334–331 B.C. But he did not live long. He died of malaria and syphilis at age thirty-two, lamenting that there were no more worlds to conquer. During the final years of his life, Alexander spent as much time indulging his passion for sex, immoral conduct, and alcohol as he did in destroying his foes. In the end, Alexander's true enemy lay within.

*Alexander the Great had
conquered the outside world
but had failed to deal with
the demons within.*

The Alexander Complex

Again the Bible is completely accurate as it predicts the events of Alexander's demise, describing in detail the "four horns" that replaced the single broken horn between the goat's eyes. These four horns represent the four generals who would later divide the sum of Alexander's great conquests among themselves: Ptolemy became master of Egypt, Cyrene, Cyprus, and Palestine; Seleucus grabbed Syria, Babylonia, and the southern area of Asia Minor; Cassander took possession of Macedonia and Greece; while Lysimachus became the uncontested ruler of Thrace and western Asia Minor.

As I ponder Alexander the Great's abbreviated life, I recall the story of a newspaper reporter who went to a nursing home to interview one of the senior patients. The reporter was surprised to see that the gentleman looked so young. He asked the standard question: "To what do you attribute your long life?" The man looked the reporter in the eye and said, "Son, I drink a lot of whiskey, and I live a very promiscuous life. I smoke a box of cigars every other day, and do just about anything I want—everything the world calls wrong." The reporter, taking notes furiously, asked, "Well, sir, you've got to tell me: how old are you?" The man replied, "Thirty-two." This man, like Alexander the Great, figured he had the world on a string, but when the string suddenly broke sin found him out, and sin won. Alexander the Great had conquered the outside world but had failed to deal with the demons within.

Enter the Madmen

Now the plot thickens, providing us with a prophecy that should make anyone who doubts the veracity of the Book of Daniel a believer. As Daniel watched the vision unfold before his eyes, there came out yet another horn—a fifth horn. It started small, but quickly grew to great influence and power toward the south, the east, and the "Beautiful Land."

Remember, Daniel's vision was describing events that would not take place for another two centuries, yet the prediction is accurate down to the very person described, Antiochus IV, also known as Epiphanes, the eighth ruler of the Seleucid division of the expanded Greek empire. Since he did not possess a legitimate right to the throne, Antiochus stooped to bribery and chicanery to become king, and what a cruel monarch he was. He was a madman—one of the two we'll speak of in this chapter. His anti-Semitism ran high. He hated God's chosen people as no ruler had ever hated them. Why did this tyrant take center stage in Daniel's vision? For two reasons: First, to remind us that almighty God knows—in minute detail—what will happen in history. Antiochus really did appear on the scene, he really did hate the Jews, and he really was the cruelest, most diabolical king anyone could imagine. But there is a second reason why Antiochus is mentioned here: Antiochus Epiphanes is a symbol of the Antichrist and how he will act during the time of the Tribulation. Remember, the little horn of chapter seven is the actual Antichrist; the little horn in chapter eight is the Jew-hater Antiochus Epiphanes, a photocopy of the Antichrist of the Tribulation. That's why we can use the texts in chapter eight to document the desecration the Antichrist will bring upon the house of Israel during the time of the end.

The Great Masquerade

Let's look further at the arrogance of this man—symbol of the Antichrist—who magnifies himself as the prince of the host, that is, prince of the Jewish people. He would glorify himself as their prince—just as Jesus Christ will one day reign as their King—again, an end-time hint that the Antichrist will also do his best to "appear as Christ" in what will be one of the greatest masquerade attempts of all time. Second Thessalonians 2:4 says that the Antichrist "opposeth and exalteth himself above all that is called God, or that is worshipped; so that he as God sitteth in the temple of God, showing himself that he is God." This comparison is an absolute match between Antiochus Epiphanes and the Antichrist.

While some Jews would go along with Antiochus' treachery—feeling they might con their way to independence by toadying up to the tyrant—they would soon discover they had backed the wrong candidate, their hypocrisy soon coming back to bite them. Even as these Jewish "turncoats" were hoping for the best deal they could strike with their foreign intruder, Antiochus began his slaughter of more than one hundred thousand Jews, demanding that the temporary survivors of his holocaust substitute heathen idols for the one, true God. He tore up their law, defiled their women, desecrated their Sabbath, had circumcised babies hanged, and forced Jews to sacrifice a sow on the holy altar of the temple. He removed the candlestick of light, the censers of gold, the veil, and the crowns and golden ornaments that adorned the temple. He scaled off mountains of gold for his own amusement and stripped the temple of everything that held significance for the Jews. He laughed in the face of the God of the Hebrews as he commanded that coins be stamped with the inscription: *Epiphanes—God!* Such blasphemy then—or now—does not go unpunished.

> *This madman's behavior is*
> *but a mild warning of the*
> *activities of the Antichrist*
> *yet to appear—who will*
> *arrive on the world scene*
> *sooner than most imagine.*

The Signs of Things to Come

Having accomplished his filthy deeds, Antiochus Epiphanes continued to supervise one of the greatest massacres of all time, boasting of his actions at every possible moment. If you would like to know more of this man's reign of terror, read the Book of Maccabees 1:29–64. This madman's behavior is but a mild warning of the activities of the Antichrist yet to appear—who will arrive on the world scene sooner than most imagine. Amazingly, Antiochus Epiphanes actually enjoyed a degree of acceptance in the early days of his reign, as we've noted, by those hypocrites willing to go along with him for their own gain—even as the Antichrist will dupe millions of our world's people with his charisma and international leadership skills. In the time of the end, this "beast" will make a peace contract with Israel, but in the middle of the peace process, he will break his word and rescind the treaty. Daniel 9:27 says, "And he shall confirm the covenant with many for one week: and in the midst of the week he shall cause the sacrifice and the oblation to cease."

Antichrist—Temporarily in Control

This breaking of the peace is a significant time in history, for now those with eyes to see will observe that the Antichrist has, in fact, become the devil incarnate. Just as Jesus was God in human form, this Antichrist, during the second three and one-half years of the Tribulation, will have Satan living in him. That's when he will say, "I am God," just as a haughty, maniacal Antiochus stamped coins with his own image in an attempt to promote his own deity. Remember, this is what Satan has always wanted to do—to be like the most high God (Isaiah 14:12–14). That's why he was ousted out of the third heaven and why Jesus said, "I beheld Satan as lightning fall from heaven" (Luke 10:18).

We must remember that the evil one has never been success-ful. Not that he hasn't tried. You'll recall how one day, deep in the wilderness, Satan promised Jesus the world and everything in it if He'd simply bow in allegiance to him (Matthew 4). Jesus didn't take the bait. However, when we come to the time of the end, the Antichrist—the embodiment of Satan—will finally pull off his coup and become what he's always wanted to be, magnifying himself above every god, with the assistance of an international religious public relations machine that persuades most of the world that he is the man of the hour. In spite of the evil he will do, in all probability he will still become *Time* mag-azine's "Man of the Year." This is the one who one day will sit on the throne in the temple in Jerusalem, look into his mirror, admire himself for his accomplishments, smile, and tell himself, "I am God, and there is none other like me." My friend, beware of New Agers who tell you that you can become God or like a god. To be seduced by this sweet-sounding rhetoric is the sort of banal thinking—or lack of thinking—that helps to set the stage for what will happen with the advent of the Antichrist. To be forewarned is to be forearmed. The day of the arrival of the Antichrist is rapidly approaching.

Daniel's Major Concern

At this point in the vision, Daniel heard one saint (angel) ask another saint how long this little horn would be allowed to carry on its transgression of desolation—for both the sanctuary and the host to be trodden under foot. This was the key question as far as Daniel was concerned. The history of tyrants was one thing; the real issue for Daniel was how long this angst would be inflicted on his people, the Jews. The answer was twenty-three hundred days—just under six and one-half years. Again, the Bible predicted these events to the very day. Antiochus Epiphanes desecrated the temple, persecuted the Jews, and wreaked havoc on all who believed from September 6, 171 to December 25, 165 B.C., exactly twenty-three hundred days as the Bible says. But, as we will see, these twenty-three hundred days have an even greater significance as we continue to unseal the mysteries of the time of the end.

15 *And it came to pass, when I, even I Daniel, had seen the vision, and sought for the meaning, then, behold, there stood before me as the appearance of a man.*

16 *And I heard a man's voice between the banks of Ulai, which called, and said, Gabriel, make this man to understand the vision.*

17 *So he came near where I stood: and when he came, I was afraid, and fell upon my face: but he said unto me, Understand, O son of man: for at the time of the end shall be the vision.*

18 *Now as he was speaking with me, I was in a deep sleep on my face toward the ground: but he touched me, and set me upright.*

19 *And he said, Behold, I will make thee know what shall be in the last end of the indignation: for at the time appointed the end shall be.*

20 *The ram which thou sawest having two horns are the kings of Media and Persia.*

21 *And the rough goat is the king of Grecia: and the great horn that is between his eyes is the first king.*

22 *Now that being broken, whereas four stood up for it, four kingdoms shall stand up out of the nation, but not in his power.*

23 *And in the latter time of their kingdom, when the transgressors are come to the full, a king of fierce countenance, and understanding dark sentences, shall stand up.*

24 *And his power shall be mighty, but not by his own power: and he shall destroy wonderfully, and shall prosper, and practise, and shall destroy the mighty and the holy people.*

25 *And through his policy also he shall cause craft to prosper in his hand; and he shall magnify himself in his heart, and by peace shall destroy many: he shall also stand up against the Prince of princes; but he shall be broken without hand.*

26 *And the vision of the evening and the morning which was told is true: wherefore shut thou up the vision; for it shall be for many days.*

The Antichrist, symbolized by Antiochus's reign of terror, will be empowered by the dragon of Revelation 13:2—Satan.

Gabriel—Messenger from God

As Gabriel attempted to explain the details of the vision, Daniel fell to the ground—with good reason. Daniel now understood the terror that would be afflicted on his people. The historical parts of the vision were clear, concise, and to the point. But Daniel could not bear to hear about the pain his people would continue to endure. This segment of the vision was also difficult for Daniel to understand because he could not fathom "end-time" thinking.

That's when Gabriel's interpretation takes a different turn. In verse 17, the angel tells Daniel that his vision refers to "the time of the end," and in verse 19 "the appointed time of the end." It doesn't get any better for the Jews, but Daniel now at least understands that there is an end-time significance to what Gabriel is telling him. This is the time when the Tribulation will be in full force—that period of history when a "time of indignation" will fall on the heads of the Jews because of their hard-hearted rebellion against God. What Gabriel is saying is this: Daniel, the indignation that began around 730 B.C. will continue through to the second coming of Jesus Christ. Gabriel is saying, "This is not for now . . . it's not for your lifetime, Daniel. It's going to be at the time of the end." Verse 23 is the strongest proof that Antiochus represents the Antichrist, and that the latter portion of the vision is not for Daniel's time, because the events in this text will not occur for one hundred years after the death of Antiochus Epiphanes.

Then the Antichrist, symbolized by Antiochus's reign of terror, will be empowered by the dragon of Revelation 13:2—Satan. He will be a proud man, the great, final ruler of the revived Roman confederacy, subduing all who stand before him, making himself a master of the world. He destroys both the mighty and the holy as he employs tactics of deceit and treachery. He dupes the world with his peace proposal, and toward the close of his rule destroys millions because they dis-covered that he was not what he claimed to be. He will offer himself as the prince of peace (Daniel 11:21, 24). However, that designation is reserved only for our Lord Jesus Christ (Isaiah 9:6). Still, the Antichrist does his best to pull off his charade of imitating Christ until the bitter end—even riding on a kingly white horse (Revelation 6:2) because he knows that Jesus the King will also ride on a white horse (Revelation 19:11). The one is faithless and vile; the other faithful and true. In the end, how-ever, this terrible Antichrist shall be "broken without hand." Again we see a prophetic parallel: Antiochus did not die at the hands of his enemies. He died of grief and remorse and went insane in Babylon, having just been defeated in the siege of Elymais and unable to bear the self-destructive impact of losing such an important battle. In like manner, the Antichrist will not die by the hand of his enemies after Satan incarnates his body. Instead, he will be destroyed by Christ at His second coming (2 Thessalonians 2:8). Finally, this personification of evil is cast into a "lake of fire burning with brimstone" (Revelation 19:20).

Daniel's heart was broken because he saw the terrible days still to come upon his people, the Jews.

Daniel's Broken Heart

The final words of Gabriel are an attempt to comfort God's frightened servant. He reminds Daniel that the Antichrist is not going to rule in his lifetime, but at the time of the end—when his predictions will finally be unsealed and revealed. For that reason Daniel was ordered to preserve the message of his vision in written form so that future generations would be able to make sense of the events when they transpired. This is why the Book of Daniel is so crucial to our understanding of events yet to come. These end-time prophecies, spoken on our behalf by a holy God, would not be understood until they began to be fulfilled—a sequence of events that began with the formation of the European Union, with Israel becoming a nation, and with Jerusalem being captured by the Israeli Army, June 5–10, 1967. Daniel himself could not grasp all of these latter-day prophecies because they would remain sealed mysteries until the time of the end.

27 *And I Daniel fainted, and was sick certain days; afterward I rose up, and did the king's business; and I was astonished at the vision, but none understood it.*

When you receive the news of an impending disaster, you know how you feel: sick to your stomach, unable to eat, and perhaps not able to pray. But then, you pull yourself together, deal with the problem, and go back to work. That's what happened to Daniel. He was so emotionally drained by his vision and Gabriel's interpretation that he lay sick upon his bed for many days. Finally, after longing for greater understanding—and praying for Jews who would be born and who would suffer long after his death—he arose and returned to his duties as a minister of the king.

Even after Gabriel's interpretation of the vision, Daniel still did not understand every detail fully, even as you and I will never completely fathom the great depths of every prophecy until they are unsealed and revealed at the time of the end. The chapter concludes with a text that implies Daniel remained puzzled for many days to come, during which time he mulled over the words of Gabriel repeatedly. With all this swirling turmoil within, Daniel comes before his God with a contrite spirit and prayer of true repentance, approaching God as *Adonai*—Lord and Master—trusting the Almighty to do what's right with his unanswered questions concerning the future. Soon he'll prove his sincerity by the wearing of sackcloth and ashes, the wonderful, heart-warming message of chapter nine.

❧9❧

God's Ultimate Program for Israel

WHAT YOU ARE about to read is a reflection on one of the most important chapters in the Book of Daniel, and one of the most remarkable passages in all of the Bible. Its dual theme of prayer and prophecy is like no other portion of God's Word: Daniel's prayer stands as a model for any person serious about seeking the Lord and His holiness in his or her life; while the prophecy of the seventy weeks contains the most precise information in Scripture that Jesus of Nazareth is the Messiah promised to the children of Israel through their own prophets.

DANIEL 9:1–2

1 *In the first year of Darius the son of Ahasuerus, of the seed of the Medes, which was made king over the realm of the Chaldeans;*

2 *In the first year of his reign I Daniel understood by books the number of the years, whereof the word of the LORD came to Jeremiah the prophet, that he would accomplish seventy years in the desolations of Jerusalem.*

Daniel is starting to do his math, and he's doing it by looking at God's timetable for the restoration of Israel. He reads in Jeremiah 25:11–12, "And this whole land shall be a desolation, and an astonishment; and these nations shall serve the king of Babylon seventy years. And it shall come to pass, when seventy years are accomplished, that I will punish the king of Babylon, and that nation, saith the LORD, for their iniquity, and the land of the Chaldeans, and will make it perpetual desolations." Daniel certainly turned to his Hebrew manuscripts to study 2 Chronicles 36, where he observed that the Jews, because they failed to protect their land (breaking seventy sabbatical years) would be punished for a period equal to their disobedience. The more Daniel read, the more excited he must have felt, because he calculated that the seventy years of judgment on his people had almost come to an end (the captivity of the Jews had started in 605 B.C. and now it was the year 538 B.C.) and that the Jews would soon be allowed to return to their home. But we are forced to say, "Not so fast, Daniel. You have only a partial understanding of what is still to come." And it is this still-to-come end-time information that is the essence of chapter nine:

> 3 And I set my face unto the Lord God, to seek by
> prayer and supplications, with fasting, and sackcloth,
> and ashes:
>
> 4 And I prayed unto the LORD my God, and made my
> confession, and said, O Lord, the great and dreadful
> God, keeping the covenant and mercy to them that
> love him, and to them that keep his commandments;
>
> 5 We have sinned, and have committed iniquity, and
> have done wickedly, and have rebelled, even by
> departing from thy precepts and from thy judgments:

6 Neither have we hearkened unto thy servants the
   prophets, which spake in thy name to our kings, our
   princes, and our fathers, and to all the people of the
   land.

7 O Lord, righteousness belongeth unto thee, but unto
   us confusion of faces, as at this day; to the men of
   Judah, and to the inhabitants of Jerusalem, and unto
   all Israel, that are near, and that are far off, through
   all the countries whither thou hast driven them,
   because of their trespass that they have trespassed
   against thee.

8 O LORD, to us belongeth confusion of face, to our
   kings, to our princes, and to our fathers, because we
   have sinned against thee.

9 To the Lord our God belong mercies and forgivenesses,
   though we have rebelled against him;

10 Neither have we obeyed the voice of the LORD our
   God, to walk in his laws, which he set before us by
   his servants the prophets.

11 Yea, all Israel have transgressed thy law, even by
   departing, that they might not obey thy voice; therefore the curse is poured upon us, and the oath that is
   written in the law of Moses the servant of God,
   because we have sinned against him.

12 And he hath confirmed his words, which he spake
   against us, and against our judges that judged us, by
   bringing upon us a great evil: for under the whole
   heaven hath not been done as hath been done upon
   Jerusalem.

13 *As it is written in the law of Moses, all this evil is come upon us: yet made we not our prayer before the Lord our God, that we might turn from our iniquities, and understand thy truth.*

14 *Therefore hath the* LORD *watched upon the evil, and brought it upon us: for the* LORD *our God is righteous in all his works which he doeth: for we obeyed not his voice.*

15 *And now, O Lord our God, that hast brought thy people forth out of the land of Egypt with a mighty hand, and hast gotten thee renown, as at this day; we have sinned, we have done wickedly.*

16 *O Lord, according to all thy righteousness, I beseech thee, let thine anger and thy fury be turned away from thy city Jerusalem, thy holy mountain: because for our sins, and for the iniquities of our fathers, Jerusalem and thy people are become a reproach to all that are about us.*

17 *Now therefore, O our God, hear the prayer of thy servant, and his supplications, and cause thy face to shine upon thy sanctuary that is desolate, for the Lord's sake.*

18 *O my God, incline thine ear, and hear; open thine eyes, and behold our desolations, and the city which is called by thy name: for we do not present our supplications before thee for our righteousnesses, but for thy great mercies.*

19 *O Lord, hear; O Lord, forgive; O Lord, hearken and do; defer not, for thine own sake, O my God: for thy city and thy people are called by thy name.*

Daniel's Prayer

Daniel begins his long prayer with a contrite and broken heart as he addresses God as *Adonai*—Sovereign Ruler. The word *Adonai* shows Daniel's recognition of God's absolute authority and power, a fitting expression for Daniel to use as he begins his litany of confession and plea for personal and national forgiveness. However, in verse 2, Daniel suddenly changes his name for God and begins to use the term *Yahweh*—which refers to God as a gracious, covenant-keeping God, holy, just, righteous, and loving. He uses the name *Yahweh* seven times, in verses 2, 4, 10, 13, 14, and 20. It's amazing that Daniel would use God's holy name in the first place because the Jews never pronounced the name of God because their reverence for the almighty God was so great. That's why they used what is called the tetragrammaton, Y-H-W-H—four letters that cannot be pronounced, and only become the word *Yahweh* when the vowels *a* and *e* are added. As we study Daniel's prayer it will become obvious why he used the term *Yahweh*, particularly as it relates to God as a covenant-keeping God, the topic which most interested Daniel since he'd now become a one-person spokesman for the plight of the Jews and was relying on the trustworthiness of the most high God to keep His promises. However, as we said before, Daniel still did not have all the information to work out all the details of God's plan because most of the predictions would only be revealed at the time of the end (Daniel 12:4).

The Jews had been scattered abroad. What was once their home had become the domicile of heathen kingdoms and pagan rulers.

As Daniel bowed before the Lord, his heart was filled with sadness for his own sin and the sins of his people. He fasted, wore sackcloth, and put ashes on his body to show his humble spirit. He was alone with God. No distractions. No interruptions. I encourage you to read and reread Daniel's prayer, because it is a model for any Christian. Even though Daniel was an upright, faithful, godly man, he still confessed that he had also sinned. Because of his tender heart toward God and a conscience that could be quickly and easily touched, he was unusually responsive when he heard the word of the Lord. Being sensitive to the Spirit of God also increased his sensitivity to the predicament of his people, the Jews, as he recited the various ways in which they rebelled against God, failed to obey His voice, refused to walk in His laws, and chose not to obey His commands. Daniel recognized that for these reasons, the curse had been poured out upon them.

The Diaspora

The Jews had been scattered across the world. What was once their home had become the domicile of heathen kingdoms and pagan rulers. Daniel knew the reason for this dispersion—the Diaspora. Deuteronomy 11:26–28 states, "Behold, I set before you this day a blessing and a curse; A blessing, if ye obey the commandments of the LORD your God, which I command you this day: And a curse, if ye will not obey the commandments of the LORD your God, but turn aside out of the way which I command you this day, to go after other gods, which ye have not known." Not only did the Jews refuse to obey the Ten Commandments found in Exodus 20, but they'd also turned their backs on the 613 other commandments given to the people of Israel. As Daniel reflects on the history of how the Jews got mired in their present dilemma, he continues to hope and pray that *Yahweh* will end the seventy years of punishment on schedule (as he, Daniel, saw it), and bring peace and relief to their sinful, troubled hearts.

Daniel's Prayer Is Also Personal

Daniel is not revising history. He is seeing history as it is, asserting that God was righteous for what He did to the Jews, admitting that we—Daniel and his people—were the culprits . . . we were the transgressors . . . we didn't obey God's voice . . . we failed to keep His commandments. His prayer was not a whining exercise to get God to overlook the past sins of His people, but a prayer of love and intercession for national and personal forgiveness, and a contrite heart, reminiscent of the words of the psalmist who prayed in Psalm 51:10, "Create in me a clean heart, O God; and renew a right spirit within me." Daniel refused to offer excuses for Israel's behavior.

Again, I urge you to read this prayer over and over, because each time you allow Daniel's heart of confession to intertwine with your own, you will be blessed and encouraged in your own Christian walk. Unfortunately, for many modern Christians the idea of true and honest confession is a lost spiritual art. But unless we recapture this spirit of humility, face up to what we've done to distance ourselves from God, and choose to make amends, our own spirits will remain shallow and insensitive to the work that God wants to do in our lives. That's why it is always in our spiritual best interest to spend time reading and applying such verses as Psalm 66:18–20, "If I regard iniquity in my heart, the Lord will not hear me: But verily God hath heard me; he hath attended to the voice of my prayer. O Blessed be God, which hath not turned away my prayer, nor his mercy from me." These verses are amplified by what we read in Isaiah 59:1–2, "Behold, the LORD's hand is not shortened, that it cannot save; neither his ear heavy, that it cannot hear: But your iniquities have separated between you and your God, and your sins have hid his face from you, that he will not hear." There is a direct correlation between our unconfessed iniquities and God's blessing for our lives—to the extent that God cannot even hear our cries if repentance is sidetracked. Daniel knew this. That's why his prayer is so powerful, a model for us to follow today. Daniel walked close to God, and the closer he walked, the more he saw the imperfections in himself and in his people because the Spirit of God lived in him.

20 *And whiles I was speaking, and praying, and confessing my sin and the sin of my people Israel, and presenting my supplication before the LORD my God for the holy mountain of my God;*

21 *Yea, whiles I was speaking in prayer, even the man Gabriel, whom I had seen in the vision at the beginning, being caused to fly swiftly, touched me about the time of the evening oblation.*

22 *And he informed me, and talked with me, and said, O Daniel, I am now come forth to give thee skill and understanding.*

23 *At the beginning of thy supplications the commandment came forth, and I am come to show thee; for thou art greatly beloved: therefore understand the matter, and consider the vision.*

24 *Seventy weeks are determined upon thy people and upon thy holy city, to finish the transgression, and to make an end of sins, and to make reconciliation for iniquity, and to bring in everlasting righteousness, and to seal up the vision and prophecy, and to anoint the most Holy.*

25 *Know therefore and understand, that from the going forth of the commandment to restore and to build Jerusalem unto the Messiah the Prince shall be seven weeks, and threescore and two weeks: the street shall be built again, and the wall, even in troublous times.*

26 *And after threescore and two weeks shall Messiah be cut off, but not for himself: and the people of the prince that shall come shall destroy the city and the sanctuary; and the end thereof shall be with a flood, and unto the end of the war desolations are determined.*

27 *And he shall confirm the covenant with many for one week: and in the midst of the week he shall cause the sacrifice and the oblation to cease, and for the over-spreading of abominations he shall make it desolate, even until the consummation, and that determined shall be poured upon the desolate.*

Astronauts would have to travel for forty thousand years at terrific speeds to get to the first star. . . . just the first leg of their inter-galactic journey if they traveled onward to the third heaven—God's throne.

The Third Heaven

As Daniel prayed, the angel Gabriel suddenly appeared before him, offering comfort and understanding to Daniel's troubled heart. Gabriel's purpose was to bring an end to

Daniel's inner confusion by imparting to him a new revelation from God. The angel began his conversation by saying something you and I should want to hear more than any other phrase in our language: "For thou art greatly loved." Daniel was concluding his prayer when he was surprised by joyous words from God. To have a greater appreciation of this scenario, consider this: Gabriel had been in the third heaven (2 Corinthians 12:2–3). That's billions of light years away—farther than our minds can grasp—and yet Gabriel now stands before Daniel, arriving in a flash—in nanoseconds.

Here's just how far Gabriel flew to arrive at Daniel's side. We're told that our astronauts would have to travel for forty thousand years at terrific speeds to get to the first star. But that would be just the first leg of their inter-galactic journey if they traveled onward to the third heaven—God's throne. There are billions, trillions, quadrillions, and quintillions of stars beyond that as we go higher and higher. To confound us yet further, scientists have now discovered a new quasar that is some eighty-two trillion billion miles out in space. And it becomes even more mindboggling. We know that light travels at a rate of 186,000 miles per second, so when a scientist talks about a "light year," that's the speed light travels at that velocity for twelve consecutive months, or a distance of six trillion miles. Now stay with me. You and I could travel thirteen and one-half billion light years and still not arrive at the third heaven—God's throne. It's incomprehensible. Just as Gabriel moved from the dimension of the third heaven to Daniel's side in an instant, so will we be able to move, at the speed of light, in our glorified bodies as we sweep through space—identical to the speed angels traverse the heavenlies.

The Significance of the Seventy Weeks

In this new revelation delivered by Gabriel, Daniel learned, sadly, that God would continue to punish Israel for at least seventy more sevens of years beyond the end of the Babylonian captivity—a number that gives us, as noted earlier, the only Old Testament prophecy that speaks of the precise hour of Messiah's first coming. It's fascinating that it was to be Gabriel who, several centuries later, would also deliver the good news of Messiah's conception and birth to a young virgin by the name of Mary (Luke 1:26–38). We now come to one the most important prophecies in all of Scripture—a prediction to be applied exclusively to Israel and to the holy city of Jerusalem. First, let's look at the meaning of the phrase, "Seventy weeks are determined upon thy people." The amount of actual time covered by this prophecy is 490 years—literally, seventy sevens. The question from scholars has always been, *Are these 490 "units" of time years, days, months, or weeks?* The math only works if these units are seen as "years." So for this prophecy to be fulfilled, Messiah would have to arrive—for the first time— before the 490 "units" would end. Remember that the 490 years began in 445 B.C.

> *"We're going to lose money,*
> *so let's not listen to God.*
> *We'll go ahead and plow*
> *and plant on the seventh*
> *year, regardless of what God*
> *or the law tells us to do."*

Now this question: What was the purpose of the 70 weeks of chastisement? The Jews had a Sabbath day which they were to honor by law. They had the freedom to work for six days, and then rest on the Sabbath, just as God had patterned His work of creation. He created the world in six days (Genesis 1:31), and rested on the seventh day (Genesis 2:2). However, the Jews not only had sabbatical days on the seventh day of the week, but they also celebrated sabbatical years. According to Leviticus 25:1–7 they were to let their land lie fallow—unused, unplanted—every seventh year. But in their greed they said in their hearts something to the effect, "This is not a very good deal for us. We're going to lose money, so let's not listen to God. We'll go ahead and plow and plant and harvest on the seventh year, regardless of what God or the law tells us to do." Because of their spiritual treachery, the Jewish people paid dearly for their 490 years of disobedience. God chastened the Jews by sending them into cruel bondage for the equivalent of seventy sabbatical years—a total of 490 years—according to the 360-day Jewish calendar. Jeremiah predicted this judgment of seventy years falling on the Jews in Jeremiah 25:9–11 when he wrote:

> Behold, I will send and take all the families of the north, saith the LORD, and Nebuchadnezzar the king of Babylon, my servant, and will bring them against this land, and against the inhabitants thereof, and against all these nations round about, and will utterly destroy them, and make them an astonishment, and an hissing, and perpetual desolations. Moreover I will take from them the voice of mirth, and the voice of gladness, the voice of the bridegroom, and the voice of the bride, the sound of the millstones, and the light of the candle. And this whole land shall be a desolation, and an astonishment; and these nations shall serve the king of Babylon seventy years.

The die was now cast. Israel would be punished during those seventy weeks (490 years)—a punishment that would be administered because of the following reasons (Daniel 9:24):

1. **"To finish the transgression."** As we've already noted, the Jews did not allow the land to rest for seventy sabbaticals—a

490 year period. Now when Messiah comes, He restores them to their land permanently. They were removed from the land as the transgression required, but now He returns to settle the debt, and provides for His people permanent restoration. Zechariah 13:1 says, "In that day there shall be a fountain opened to the house of David and to the inhabitants of Jerusalem for sin and for uncleanness."

2. **"To make an end of sins."** The corporate sins of the nation of Israel will come to an end at the second coming of Jesus Christ. The Jews, as all other people, have sinned, and their transgressions would be paid for by the blood of Jesus shed at Calvary. Because this provision has been made, Messiah comes to announce that the sin that brought all the judgment upon them has been removed (Hebrews 10:17).

3. **"To make reconciliation for iniquity."** During this seventy-week period, God has made redemption available through the sacrificial death and resurrection of Jesus Christ. Zechariah 12:10 says, "And I will pour upon the house of David, and upon the inhabitants of Jerusalem, the spirit of grace and of supplications: and they shall look upon me whom they have pierced, and they shall mourn for him, as one mourneth for his only son, and shall be in bitterness for him, as one that is in bitterness for his firstborn."

4. **"And to bring in everlasting righteousness."** This speaks of the return of Christ at the end of the 490 years. At this time He establishes His kingdom, returning as King of Kings and Lord of Lords. Finally, the world becomes a wonderful place, described in joyful terms in Isaiah 35:8: "And an highway shall be there, and a way, and it shall be called The way of holiness; the unclean shall not pass over it; but it shall be for those: the wayfaring men, though fools, shall not err therein." This is what Revelation 21:27 speaks of when it refers to this holy city that hovers above the earth. It is a place of righteousness.

Nothing can enter that defiles or makes the celestial city unholy. The message here is this: We cannot—and will not—have a perfect world until Jesus comes and binds Satan for a thousand years.

5. **"To seal up the vision and prophecy."** Daniel was instructed to seal the vision until the time of the end. Now—as you read these words—we are approaching that time, and for that reason we're able to explain it, unseal it, and see its depth with Spirit-led understanding. I trust you are catching a glimpse of just how close we are to that great day. Until now—for centuries, actually—we have struggled to see through a darkened glass, but now the truth of Daniel's vision is becoming clearer by the day. We are not at the final time yet, but we are getting very close. Then, once Messiah returns, prophecy will be forever finished because there will be nothing left to predict. The Son of Man—the radiant Lord Jesus Christ—will be in our midst, and all prophecy will be sealed permanently.

6. **"To anoint the most Holy."** This is a reference to Ezekiel chapters 41–46, where the prophet talks about the anointing of the Holy of Holies in the "millennial" temple. When the Lord Jesus returns, *Yahweh* the Father says, "I set my king upon my holy hill of Zion" (Psalm 2:6). Just as God's priests in the Old Testament and His servants in the New Testament were anointed for holy service, so Jesus Christ the Prince—the King of Kings—will be anointed for the centuries to come.

At this point I'm going to quote a verse that is the greatest prophecy ever recorded, proving that God alone could have written this book. Why? Because we now come to the exact day that is prophesied in these texts. Verse 25 reads, "Know therefore and understand, that from the going forth of the commandment to restore and to build Jerusalem unto the Messiah the Prince shall be seven weeks, and threescore and two weeks:

the street shall be built again, and the wall, even in troublous times."

Let's review the significance of this verse in the context of Nehemiah 2:1-8 where we learn that some of the Jews who had visited their homeland were disturbed because their nation was in such disarray. That's why they requested that the city of Jerusalem—including the wall—be rebuilt. With that background, let's consider Nehemiah 2:1 to investigate the chronology of dates mentioned. "And it came to pass in the month Nisan, in the twentieth year of Artaxerxes the king. . . ." *The Encyclopedia Britannica* says this king came to power in 465 B.C. But now it's Artaxerxes' twentieth year of rule, which takes us down to 445 B.C. Here's the arithmetic: 465 minus 20 = 445 B.C. This is the month Nisan, but no date is given. That is not, however, an issue because Jewish custom tells us that whenever there is no date we are to assume it is always the first day. This means it is the first day of Nisan, 445 B.C. Translated into our modern calendar, that's March 14, 445 B.C. That is the beginning point of the rebuilding of the wall and city of Jerusalem—a task that had to be completed in "seven weeks" or, literally, forty-nine years. And it happened right on schedule.

King Jesus Will Reign

However, there is a second part to this prophecy that refers to the presentation of Jesus Christ as King. Note there are two princes in this text: The first is Jesus, who will reign as the Prince of Peace (Isaiah 9:6). The second prince is a Roman general who invades Jerusalem. Here, we are talking about the first Prince—Jesus Christ—who will be "cut off" after seven weeks and sixty-two weeks, for a total of sixty-nine weeks, or 483 years. Now, we take the 483 years and multiply it by the Jewish method of reckoning—which is 360 days in a year. Do you know what 483 times 360 is? 173,880 days. From the date that Nehemiah said, "You may go ahead and rebuild your wall and Jerusalem" (March 14, 445 B.C.) to the day that Jesus Christ rode into Jerusalem on the foal of a donkey (April 6, 32 A.D.) exactly 173,880 days had passed. Now do you believe that prophecy is right on? If the Jews had only studied their Old Testament prophecy, they would have known that Jesus was their Messiah.

> *Day 173,880 was the crowning day, and Jewish minds did not grasp it—nor did they accept their Messiah.*

This is why Jesus said to His people, the Jews, in Luke 19:42, "If thou hadst known, even thou, at least in this thy day, the things which belong unto thy peace! but now they are hidden from thine eyes." Day 173,880 was the crowning day, and Jewish minds did not grasp it—nor did they accept their Messiah. If God could prove—as we've just outlined—the precise arrival of Jesus into Jerusalem, is there any question that the remainder of the prophecies in the Book of Daniel will be fulfilled?

As we come to the close of this most important prophetic chapter in the Bible, we also need to deal with the content of verse 26 that speaks of the prince who will come to destroy the city and the sanctuary. This prince was Vespasian and his son Titus—Roman generals who in 70 A.D. marched on Jerusalem and murdered hundreds of thousands of Jews, again destroying the city. Here we see a similarity between the treachery of this father and son and an earlier tyrant Antiochus Epiphanes, because all three are types of the Antichrist who will rise to power in the last days. But here Vespasian and Titus are highlighted because they are Roman princes. Later, the Antichrist will come as an international leader out of a revived Roman Empire that is presently expanding and wielding influence just as Daniel predicted. For this and many more reasons—all documented by God's Word—we are dogmatic when we say that our era of time could definitely be what Daniel called "the time of the end."

Now what about the apparent "gap" that exists between verses 26 and 27—a gap of some two thousand years? This is an important period of time, because without it, we would be forced to see these events taking place within a limited period of 490 days, instead of 490 years. The former would be impossible. There are skeptics who scoff that a gap between these verses is a man-made theory. However, the Bible states emphatically that there will be a period of time—a gap—between Jesus' first and second coming. Isaiah 9:6 says, "Unto us a child is born" (the virgin birth); "unto us a Son is given and the government shall be upon his shoulder" (the government was not upon His shoulder the first time He came to Jerusalem). When Jesus Christ comes again—the second time—that's when the government will be upon His shoulder, as He rules and reigns as King of Kings and Lord of Lords for a period of one thousand years (Revelation 20:4).

By the time we reach verse 27, the Antichrist is already in full power, and Daniel's seventieth week is in effect. It begins when this evil one confirms his peace contract with Israel. This is the start of the seventieth week, and the beginning of the seven-year period of Tribulation. The Antichrist deceives a gullible world by confirming the covenant with many—first with Israel—for one week, one *shabua*—or seven years. The information I am about to present is vitally important. If the first sixty-nine weeks, or *shabuas,* total 483 years or 173,880 days on the Jewish calendar annually, and this prophecy was fulfilled in every detail on the final day—then the final week or Hebrew *shabua,* the last seven-year period of 2,520 days, will also be fulfilled right up to the exact moment. That's why Revelation 11:2 and 13:5 mention forty-two months, and Revelation 11:3 and 12:6 cite 1,260 days as one-half of the Tribulation period. Then in the middle of that *shabua*—after forty-two months—the Antichrist causes the sacrifices to cease. Antiochus Epiphanes, a predecessor and forerunner of the soon-coming global dictator, previously did this centuries ago when he stomped out the Jewish sacrifices and desecrated the Jewish temple.

The Rebuilding of the Temple

How could such an act be perpetuated in our day without the existence of a temple? Here's the answer. Israelites are talking about rebuilding the temple in our day. I encourage you to read your newspapers and weekly magazines with spiritual eyes in the days ahead because even now building materials are being gathered and temple utensils created for the rebuilding of the temple in Jerusalem. When the new temple is erected, all will go relatively well for a while, but then, midway into the Tribulation hour, the Antichrist will sit proudly on that temple throne and claim to be the world's god (2 Thessalonians 2:4). The false prophet will create an image in the likeness of the Antichrist (Revelation 13:15) and all mankind will be commanded to fall down and worship the beast of the revived Roman Empire mentioned in Daniel 7:8—just as Nebuchadnezzar commanded the people of Babylon to bow down and worship him. If, during the Tribulation period, the people do not bow to the Antichrist and give him full allegiance, they will be killed (Revelation 13:15; 20:4–5). When the pagan tyrant Antiochus Epiphanes set up his pagan deities in the place of the most high God, and put a sow on the temple altar, it was called "the abomination that maketh desolate" (Daniel 11:31; 12:11). Now, more than two thousand years later, the Antichrist will also set up an image called "the abomination of desolation" according to the statements of Jesus in Matthew 24:15 and Mark 13:14. Why? Because he is defiling God's holy temple. The Jews revere their holy temple—the Antichrist mocks it and them by breaking one of the Jews' commandments concerning the placing of an idol in the temple (Exodus 20:4–5). At this point their long sought-for temple again becomes desolate because of the abominable idol therein.

The Calm before the Storm

Jesus, in Matthew 24:15–21, says:

> When ye therefore shall see the abomination of desolation, spoken of by Daniel the prophet, stand in the holy place, (whoso readeth, let him understand:) Then let them which be in Judaea flee into the mountains: Let him which is on the housetop not come down to take any thing out of his house: Neither let him which is in the field return back to take his clothes. And woe unto them that are with child, and to them that give suck in those days! But pray ye that your flight be not in the winter, neither on the sabbath day: For then shall be great tribulation, such as was not since the beginning of the world to this time, no, nor ever shall be.

Why flee? Because Satan's final forty-two months are about to be unleashed globally, and he's filled with wrath (Revelation 12:12). Then Russia marches and the abomination of desolation (or image) is set up in the temple during this final three-and-one-half-year period known as the Great Tribulation (Revelation 7:14). It is the time of the end (Daniel 11:40; 12:4).

This revelation and interpretation of the vision delivered to Daniel by the angel Gabriel was a two-edged sword: one of gloom and doom; the other of hope. Gloom, because the Antichrist is about to appear. Hope, because Christ destroys him with the brightness of His coming (2 Thessalonians 2:8). Today, we are seeing what can only be called "the calm before the storm." History is not yet complete, but the handwriting is on the wall for those who have eyes to see.

❧ 10 ❧

Visions and Beasts No More... Daniel Sees Jesus

CHAPTER TEN OF THE Book of Daniel is the introduction to his last recorded revelation and is the first of three parts of a vision—a vision some scholars say is the greatest of all the revelations of Daniel. This chapter gives us information on something decidedly different from anything we've read as we are introduced to a special group of angels—some who harbor ill-will toward God and attempt to defeat the divine purpose as it relates to God's rule over His people, Israel, both in the present (in Daniel's time) and in the days yet to come (at the time of the end). Chapter ten is graphic in that it also provides detailed information on how Daniel received his final revelation, including many surprising incidents that accompany God's delivery of this message to Daniel.

DANIEL 10:1–3

1 *In the third year of Cyrus king of Persia a thing was revealed unto Daniel, whose name was called Belteshazzar; and the thing was true, but the time appointed was long: and he understood the thing, and had understanding of the vision.*

2 *In those days I Daniel was mourning three full weeks.*

> 3 I ate no pleasant bread, neither came flesh nor wine in
> my mouth, neither did I anoint myself at all, till three
> whole weeks were fulfilled.

Daniel's State of Mind

This last revelation received by Daniel came to him just two years after King Cyrus had officially brought the Babylonian captivity to an end by allowing the Jews to return to Israel. However, the Jews returned home without Daniel. We don't know precisely why Daniel remained behind, but we can surmise it was either because of his advancing years—now in his mid- to upper-eighties—or because he still may have had essential work to do for the Persian leadership—perhaps as a senior advisor. Therefore his presence was vital. He also may have felt that to remain behind would permit him to use his enormous influence for good as his people, the Jews, made the difficult transition to return to a land that many had never seen—or that was a fading memory.

*He knew the time of the end
would be a period of unprecedented judgment on the Jews.*

Daniel Understands the Vision

The revelation Daniel was about to receive was hard for him to hear and more difficult for him to accept, although he knew in his heart that it was true. Daniel's vision revealed an enormous conflict that would afflict his people at a later time. This would be the greatest war the world's powers had ever encountered, a future conflict that would include something unheard of before: a massive angelic invasion that, while unseen, would be instrumental in shaping the final result of international events. The most difficult part of the message for Daniel to accept was that this future trauma would threaten the very existence of Israel—a nation and people who had already suffered so much, been so long in captivity, and seemed to be on a perpetual losing streak that would play out to the time of the end. Unlike Daniel's earlier visions and dreams, he declared that he understood this one, and that he also comprehended how the events predicted would not occur during his own lifetime. Daniel, however, took little comfort in this knowledge, because his heart was so tender toward the ultimate destiny of his people.

Daniel understood that during the "seventy weeks" to come the Jews would suffer great persecution (Daniel 12:1) as the forces of Egypt, leading an Arab federation (Daniel 11:40), and a king from the North, Russia, plus kings from the East, China, and other Oriental nations (Daniel 11:44), would move in upon Israel for the bloodiest confrontation in history. Daniel knew this would take place during the seventieth week—a time period of seven years known as the "latter days" (Daniel 10:14), and referred to as "the time of the end" (Daniel 11:40; 12:4). While Daniel could not know the specifics of this terrible era of suffering yet to come, he had enough understanding to know that it would be a horrible period of history for the people of Israel. That's why this saintly prophet—loved by God—is so moved that he mourns at the thought of what is going to happen to his people. He knew the time of the end would be a period of unprecedented judgment on the Jews as the nations of the world would move against his people, and particularly against Jerusalem (Zechariah 14:2).

> *Had the Jews not suffered*
> *enough? And had God not*
> *made a promise to relieve them*
> *of their pain at the close of the*
> *seventy years of captivity?*

When Daniel received the first part of this final revelation, he had been fasting for twenty-one days. Daniel was so focused on remaining humble before God that he kept himself in a constant state of alert so he would be ready to hear the word of the Lord. It's quite possible that Daniel was still grieving—and therefore fasting—because of the inner turmoil he felt after the unsettling vision in chapter eight, wondering why his people would continue to suffer after the close of the seventy years of captivity. Had the Jews not suffered enough? And had God not made a promise to relieve them of their pain at the close of the seventy years of captivity? What we now see in Daniel is a progressive understanding of what was to happen in the days to come. We also see a kind, gentle old man whose sensitivity to the things of God—and to the plight of his people—remained acute: Daniel remained God's man to the very end.

4 *And in the four and twentieth day of the first month, as I was by the side of the great river, which is Hiddekel;*

5 *Then I lifted up mine eyes, and looked, and behold a certain man clothed in linen, whose loins were girded with fine gold of Uphaz:*

6 *His body also was like the beryl, and his face as the appearance of lightning, and his eyes as lamps of fire,*

and his arms and his feet like in colour to polished
brass, and the voice of his words like the voice of a
multitude.

7 *And I Daniel alone saw the vision: for the men that*
were with me saw not the vision; but a great quaking
fell upon them, so that they fled to hide themselves.

8 *Therefore I was left alone, and saw this great vision,*
and there remained no strength in me: for my comeli-
ness was turned in me into corruption, and I retained
no strength.

9 *Yet heard I the voice of his words: and when I heard*
the voice of his words, then was I in a deep sleep on
my face, and my face toward the ground.

Daniel Sees the Pre-Incarnate Christ

One day Daniel, either on a leisurely stroll or on business for the government, was standing by the Hiddekel (or Tigris) River. There he was confronted by a likeness he had never observed before. The Bible describes this figure as dressed in linen . . . with a waist girded with a belt of pure gold, a body like beryl, a face with the appearance like that of lightning, eyes like flaming torches, arms and feet of polished brass, and the sound of his voice like the sound of a tumult. Is there any doubt in our minds that such a being would capture Daniel's attention! The question, however, must be asked: Who was this heavenly being? Why was he there?

We don't need to search long for our answer because the description of this being bears a direct correspondence to the glorified Christ we read about in Revelation 1:13–15: "And in the midst of the seven candlesticks one like unto the Son of man, clothed with a garment down to the foot, and **girt about** the paps with a golden girdle. His head and his hairs were white like wool, as white as snow; and his eyes were as a flame of fire; And his feet like unto fine brass, as if they burned in a furnace; and his voice as the sound of many waters"—an almost exact description of what Daniel saw that day by the shores of the great Tigris River. Like the appearance of a fourth person in the fiery furnace, this was a Christophany—a physical appearance of the person of Jesus Christ.

Christ—the Same Yesterday, Today, and Forever

If, for some reason, Christ's eternal existence sounds far-fetched, what does one do with John 1:3, that, "All things were made by him"? Or John 1:10, "He was in the world, the world was made by him"? Or Colossians 1:16, which says, "For by Christ were all things created that are in heaven and in earth"? This may not be easy for us to understand, but whether we comprehend it or not, this is God's Holy Word. In Proverbs 30:4 we read: "Who hath ascended up into heaven, or descended? Who hath gathered the wind in his fists? Who hath bound the waters in a garment? Who hath established all the ends of the earth? What is his name, and what is his son's name, if thou canst tell?" Isn't it amazing—this text states that God had a son hundreds of years before Christ's birth at Bethlehem. We must conclude, then, that the heavenly being standing before Daniel is none other than the Lord Jesus Christ.

Daniel was not alone when he was confronted by the person of Jesus Christ. There were companions with him—but not for long. While they apparently sensed that something momentous was taking place, they were unable to withstand the dread of the moment, similar to Saul's experience on the Damascus turnpike (Acts 9:7). They, too, could do nothing but hide their faces from the glory of Christ and flee, leaving Daniel alone in his encounter with Christ. Suddenly Daniel—man among men, strong, lion-tamer, and counselor to the kings of Babylon, fell to the ground when he heard the words of the Lord. Immediately His strength was sapped, His knees buckled, and he fell into a deep sleep when the sound of thunderous, divine words—like the sound of many rushing waters—assaulted his human ears.

10 *And, behold, an hand touched me, which set me upon my knees and upon the palms of my hands.*

11 *And he said unto me, O Daniel, a man greatly beloved, understand the words that I speak unto thee, and stand upright: for unto thee am I now sent. And when he had spoken this word unto me, I stood trembling.*

12 *Then said he unto me, Fear not, Daniel: for from the first day that thou didst set thine heart to understand, and to chasten thyself before thy God, thy words were heard, and I am come for thy words.*

13 *But the prince of the kingdom of Persia withstood me one and twenty days: but, lo, Michael, one of the chief princes, came to help me; and I remained there with the kings of Persia.*

14 *Now I am come to make thee understand what shall befall thy people in the latter days: for yet the vision is for many days.*

15 *And when he had spoken such words unto me, I set my face toward the ground, and I became dumb.*

16 *And, behold, one like the similitude of the sons of men touched my lips: then I opened my mouth, and spake, and said unto him that stood before me, O my lord, by the vision my sorrows are turned upon me, and I have retained no strength.*

17 *For how can the servant of this my lord talk with this
my lord? for as for me, straightway there remained no
strength in me, neither is there breath left in me.*

Daniel Regains His Strength and Understands the Reason for Christ's Appearing

Now the scene suddenly changes. It is no longer Christ who
stands before Daniel, but an angel. There is a specific reason
for us to interpret this section of the passage in this way. If this
were still Christ speaking to Daniel, we would be forced to
conclude that Christ had little or no power, because the prince
of Persia (v. 13) who withstood the messenger would be able to
stand firmly against Christ and, therefore, demonstrate more
power than the Son of God possessed. This, of course, would
be impossible. It is therefore safe to conclude that the one now
standing before Daniel is an angel—probably Gabriel—who
again has made his incredible journey to Daniel's side from the
third heaven—an astronomical distance, described in chapter
eight. This holy messenger speaks words of comfort to this
choice servant of God.

But imagine Daniel's confusion: One moment he sees the
pre-incarnate Christ, and the next moment the angel Gabriel,
who lifted him up, and delivered a message from the Lord. The
words uttered by this heavenly being are words you and I certainly would want Jesus to say to us when that great day
arrives as we stand before Him: words of comfort, love, and
appreciation for our faithfulness to the cause of Christ during
our witness on earth. But the angel had even more to say to
Daniel. We begin to see this revelation take on a new dimension, as Gabriel speaks of the kingdom of Persia's power, and
how a demonic spirit that controlled the ruler of Persia had
"withstood" God's angel, probably Michael, for twenty-one

days. Throughout the Bible we read of many rulers of the world who are controlled by these evil, demonic spirits. In Isaiah 14:12–14, we find that Satan fell because he wanted to be like God. In Luke 10:18, Jesus said, "I saw Satan as lightning fall from heaven"—a reference to the third heaven (2 Corinthians 12:2). Today, Satan is still in control of heaven number one, and heaven number two. That's why he can approach the end of heaven number two and keep up his incessant verbal abuse of God's people—the brethren (Revelation 12:10). The Bible says that Satan is still the god of this world system . . . that he is the prince of this world (John 12:31). That's why you and I do not wrestle against flesh and blood—against other human beings—but instead against principalities, against powers, against the rulers of the darkness of this world, and against spiritual (literally, *spirit*) wickedness in high places (Ephesians 6:12).

> *But don't be afraid. Don't let your heart be upset. Your God is strong—omnipotent, or all-powerful. He is in control of the affairs of men.*

Peace . . . Not Fear

Fallen angels are everywhere, and Satan is the head of them, holding the designated title of prince of the power of the air (Ephesians 2:2). This prince of the first and second heaven, along with millions of his demonic spirits, has the ability to control political leaders. It was the prince (or ruler) of ancient Persia who was controlled by one of these demonic agents. This enemy of mankind is powerful, but not all-powerful. Ultimate power and control belong to *Yahweh*. The message here is clear: "Daniel, I know that what you've heard in your visions is emotionally devastating to you. You feel sorry for your people and are saddened to realize what will happen to them in the latter days. But don't be afraid. Your God is strong—omnipotent, or all-powerful. He is in control of the affairs of men. His angels surround you, and they represent the power of your almighty God."

This sounds much like the comforting words spoken by Jesus in John 14:27, "Peace I leave with you, my peace I give unto you: not as the world giveth, give I unto you. Let not your heart be troubled, neither let it be afraid." That was the angel's message to Daniel. He wanted to remove all sense of dread from Daniel's heart. He wanted him to know that it was exclusively the enemy, Satan, who put timidity into his spirit. If he relied on the mercy and faithfulness of God, that fear would vanish (2 Timothy 1:7).

Gabriel was putting this angelic warfare into perspective: There are good angels, and there are bad angels. The angels of God stand with the Lord's people to comfort them, and hold them up when times get tough. Such angelic beings were also available to our Savior. Jesus said in Matthew 26:53, "Thinkest thou that I cannot now pray to my Father, and he shall presently give me more than twelve legions of angels?" What power—to literally snap His fingers and be able to command the arrival of twelve legions of angels, a legion in a Roman army being seven thousand men! (See also Matthew 4:11.) Hebrews 1:14 says, "Are they not all ministering spirits, sent forth to minister for them who shall be heirs of salvation?" Our guardian angels are there to protect us. They are the elect or holy angels, numbering into the millions (1 Timothy 5:21; Hebrews 12:22). On the other hand, millions of evil angels also fill the heavenlies. These are the "devils" (literally, demons or fallen angels) mentioned often in God's Word, and Satan is the prince of these demons (Matthew 9:34). Together he and his minions control the minds of leaders who are the personification of evil—the holocaust-producing Josef Stalins, Adolph Hitlers, and Idi Amins of our world. I have spoken of these heavenly beings in some depth because they are integral to our understanding of this introduction to the last revelation received by Daniel.

> *Today, with an existing European Union, a nation called Israel, and Jews in control of Jerusalem, we find ourselves with an increasing number of signs pointing to the time of the end.*

Message of the Latter Days

The message was again difficult for Daniel to hear and accept—but this time he understood it. He did not need further clarification. He knew there would be a horrendous persecution of Israel (Jeremiah 30:7; Daniel 12:1; Matthew 24:22; Revelation 12:13), and that it would occur during the latter days, a term equivalent to the time of the end. Today, with an existing European Union, a nation called Israel, and Jews in control of Jerusalem, we find ourselves with an increasing number of signs pointing to the time of the end. As you'll recall, Daniel's end-time prediction began when the prophet stated under Nebuchadnezzar's reign: "There is a God in heaven that revealeth secrets, that has sent me to tell thee, Nebuchadnezzar, what shall be in the latter days." For us moderns, the handwriting is on the wall. The seventieth week of Daniel is rapidly approaching. But the good news for believers is that prior to the beginning of the seventieth week, we will be raptured (Revelation 4:1).

At this point, Daniel fell to the ground, speechless. When he recovered, he became aware that the "lord" was standing in front of him. If you'll notice in the text the word *lord* has a small *l*. If this were deity, the word would have a capital *L* as its first letter. This means that a different angelic being has come to comfort him. Daniel's response is one of humility. He feels lowly and unworthy, not fit to stand in the presence of this holy being sent by his heavenly Father with a message of comfort, which is to "fear not."

18 *Then there came again and touched me one like the appearance of a man, and he strengthened me,*

19 *And said, O man greatly beloved, fear not: peace be unto thee, be strong, yea, be strong. And when he had spoken unto me, I was strengthened, and said, Let my lord speak; for thou hast strengthened me.*

20 *Then said he, Knowest thou wherefore I come unto thee? and now will I return to fight with the prince of Persia: and when I am gone forth, lo, the prince of Grecia shall come.*

21 *But I will shew thee that which is noted in the scripture of truth: and there is none that holdeth with me in these things, but Michael your prince.*

Daniel Regains His Strength

The angel does not give up on Daniel. He touches him again, giving him more strength as he encourages this prophet to be strong. This is as important a message for us today as it was for Daniel ages ago: Our strength comes from the Lord, and it comes by degrees. The Bible says that we should partake of His strength on a daily basis. We don't receive a month's, or a year's worth of strength instantaneously. Instead, God gives us grace for each day. That's why we are to pray without ceasing, because it is when we become lackadaisical that the "prince of the power of the air" attempts to "devour us" (1 Peter 5:8). Daniel knew he needed help, and he did not decline assistance when God sent it to him. By now, the angel had completed his mission to Daniel and asked Daniel if he understood why a heavenly being had been sent by the Father to encourage him. What kindness, patience, and compassion. I wonder if we are that loving and kind when we try to communicate Christ's gospel of love to those who are confused and doubtful about the veracity of God's Word. Perhaps we could take a lesson from this heavenly being.

At that point the angel announced his departure because he, Gabriel, needed to get back to the battle zone—but not until he was sure Daniel fully understood what God had shown him about the future of his people, the Jews. Gabriel was going to join Michael in battle against the fallen spirits controlling the ruler of Persia. Later, when the battle in the heavens would cease after defeating the demons controlling the ruler of Persia, there would be yet another skirmish with the leader of Greece. Simply stated, Medo-Persia would ultimately fall to Greece and another satanic spirit would control the ruler of this conquering nation. Isn't the Word of God amazing? This is precisely what happened, just as the angel told Daniel it would—two hundred years in advance.

There's a double meaning in the text when the angel states: There will come a time when the nations will fight again. So when will Persia again war against the Jews? When the Russian army marches against Israel, as mentioned in Ezekiel 38:1–2 and 5. Ancient Persia is known today as Iran and Iraq. Then when Russia invades Israel, the European Union leaders will say, "This simply cannot happen" (Daniel 11:40–41). Then the western forces march to try to put an end to the northern army of Russia and her allies: Egypt, the Arabs, and others. This is when we find the prince of Greece involved. How can we be sure of this? Because Greece became the tenth nation to join the European Union on January 1, 1981. The powerful revived Roman Empire, including Greece, is already beginning to form its own army—an army that will one day move with great strength into the Middle East. It will happen in our generation. The time is coming. The seals that kept the lid on the mysteries of Daniel are now coming off, and with their unsealing we see how close we have come to the time of the end.

Michael, the Warrior

Gabriel is the one who, while able to do battle, and battle well, is usually cast in the role of announcer of the message. But the archangel who leads the military hosts of heaven is Michael, and he is the one mentioned here in the Book of Daniel as well as in the Book of Revelation. One of the most significant predictions Daniel received is in 12:1 where Michael stands for (protects) the people of Israel. And when will Michael arise to do battle for the Jews? When the greatest anti-Semitic purge in history takes place, when Satan is cast out of heaven (Revelation 12:7–13). Michael will be there to fight for—and defend—God's people. Michael is that warrior angel, and Satan, once god of the heavens, loses, and is cast out. He adds woe to the inhabitants of the earth and the sea, but he knows he has limited time to do his work—only forty-two months. Half of the Tribulation period is over by then, the first half having been ruled and energized by Satan empowering the Antichrist. But now as Satan comes down to earth, he incarnates the body of Antichrist, and this world leader—once applauded by the world's nations and people—goes berserk. What does he try to do? He attempts to obliterate every Jew on the earth. Revelation 12:13 states: "He persecutes the woman who brought forth the man child." This woman is Mary, the Jewish virgin who depicts the greatest anti-Semitic onslaught in history. Nevertheless, the good news is that there will be a time of victory, and the archangel Michael will be in the middle of the fray. Michael is going to win the final battle, because the Lord intervenes. He stops the terrorism being inflicted on the Jewish people and saves them from their distress. Jeremiah 30:7 and Daniel 12:1 talk about their glorious day of deliverance, a great day that is yet to come. Even now, we pray for the peace of Israel, because they who do shall prosper (Psalm 122:6). Following this time, Christ descends to begin His thousand-year reign upon earth, and Michael rids the world of its vilest enemy. Revelation 20:1–2 says, "I saw an angel come down from heaven, having the key of the bottomless pit and a great chain in his hand. And he laid hold on the dragon, that old serpent, which is the Devil, and Satan, and bound him a thousand years."

Amazing mysteries have been revealed in chapter ten, but the vision is only partially unsealed to our eyes. As we now move on to the final two chapters of Daniel, angelic beings persevere in providing us with information about the time of the end and how the role of our Savior and Lord Jesus Christ—and legions of angels—will continue to intervene in the affairs of men and women everywhere. Behind the head-lines of CNN, the believer can be assured that God remains in control of our world as international events unfold—circumstances we will grasp more fully as we peel back more mysteries hidden for centuries.

·11·

History Ends . . . Prophecy Begins

THE GREAT REFORMER John Calvin (1509–1564) was so overwhelmed with the historical accuracy of Daniel's prophecy in the first part of chapter eleven that he wrote forty pages of commentary describing in minute detail the future exploits of each world leader, the battles engaged, and the ensuing intrigue. In fact, the meticulous and historically accurate nature of these verses has persuaded many liberal ministers to believe that Daniel could not have written this book, suggesting that no one could have been privy to so many details of forthcoming events. Therefore, they argue, the Book of Daniel must have been written much later. To that I would simply reply that since God is God, and since He knows all things, it really would not be difficult for the Almighty to fill Daniel with His Holy Spirit and through him make known the events in history yet to come (2 Peter 1:20–21).

Some readers may want me to spend as much time as John Calvin did in delineating past predictions that have already been fulfilled in the first part of chapter eleven, perhaps hoping that I would trace the accomplishments of every king, every skirmish, and every historical circumstance in this four hundred-year period to prove there are no errors in Daniel's prophecy. However, for those who may not have as great a historical bent, this would be too much detail, since the first thirty-five verses of this chapter eleven include 135 prophecies—each completely fulfilled down to the smallest detail. Undoubtedly, delving into each of the 135 predictions would become exceedingly laborious. With those considerations in mind, I will simply sketch out a few of the completed historical events of this chapter and then spend most of the time exploring the confluence of the many events that suggest so strongly that we are now at the time of the end—a discussion which begins with verse 36.

Daniel 11:1–4

1 *Also I in the first year of Darius the Mede, even I, stood to confirm and to strengthen him.*

2 *And now will I show thee the truth. Behold, there shall stand up yet three kings in Persia; and the fourth shall be far richer than they all: and by his strength through his riches he shall stir up all against the realm of Grecia.*

3 *And a mighty king shall stand up, that shall rule with great dominion, and do according to his will.*

4 *And when he shall stand up, his kingdom shall be broken, and shall be divided toward the four winds of heaven; and not to his posterity, nor according to his dominion which he ruled: for his kingdom shall be plucked up, even for others beside those.*

> *We are not concerned with the critics' skepticism, but rather rejoice in the knowledge that we have a God who knows the future.*

Details that Confound the Skeptics

These first four verses trace the history of four Persian rulers and Alexander the Great of Greece—giving summary details of the Ptolemies of Egypt and the Seleucids of Syria, whom, as you will recall, represented the two major divisions of Alexander's worldwide kingdom. It is this kind of historical detail that confounds the skeptic who says, "How could any one—God included—have known with such accuracy the events, people, and interaction of nations four centuries before such events took place?" Here, however, we are not concerned with the critics' skepticism, but rather rejoice in the knowledge that we have a God who knows the future, has ordained its activity, and is now allowing us to unseal mysteries so long hidden from view.

Here's a quick summary of some of the enormous amount of prophetic information contained in Daniel's vision—all of which has now been fulfilled. When Daniel received his fourth revelation, Cyrus was king of Medo-Persia. However, Christ—in the vision—told Daniel there would be three more Medo-Persian rulers prior to the reign of successor number four. The three kings were Cambyses, Pseudo-Smerdis, and Darius I Hystaspes. The fourth would be Xerxes I, a powerful ruler who later accumulated great armies, power, and wealth over a four-year period which he used to invade Greece in the year 480 B.C. I highlight this here because it was Xerxes' attack of Greece that moved Alexander the Great to attack Medo-Persia some one hundred and fifty years later. However, not all would go well for Alexander in spite of his great power and dominance of so much of the then-known world. Though the young king grasped worldwide control, he soon died of malaria and syphilis at the age of thirty-two. Previously, we saw a defeated Greece predicted in the form of a leopard (Daniel 7:6), and as the goat in Daniel 8:5–6. Events prophesied; events fulfilled.

5 And the king of the south shall be strong, and one of his princes; and he shall be strong above him, and have dominion; his dominion shall be a great dominion.

6 And in the end of years they shall join themselves together; for the king's daughter of the south shall come to the king of the north to make an agreement: but she shall not retain the power of the arm; neither shall he stand, nor his arm: but she shall be given up, and they that brought her, and he that begat her, and he that strengthened her in these times.

7 But out of a branch of her roots shall one stand up in his estate, which shall come with an army, and shall enter into the fortress of the king of the north, and shall deal against them, and shall prevail:

8 And shall also carry captives into Egypt their gods, with their princes, and with their precious vessels of silver and of gold; and he shall continue more years than the king of the north.

9 So the king of the south shall come into his kingdom, and shall return into his own land.

10 But his sons shall be stirred up, and shall assemble a multitude of great forces: and one shall certainly come, and overflow, and pass through: then shall he return, and be stirred up, even to his fortress.

11 And the king of the south shall be moved with choler, and shall come forth and fight with him, even with the king of the north: and he shall set forth a great multitude; but the multitude shall be given into his hand.

12 *And when he hath taken away the multitude, his heart shall be lifted up; and he shall cast down many ten thousands: but he shall not be strengthened by it.*

13 *For the king of the north shall return, and shall set forth a multitude greater than the former, and shall certainly come after certain years with a great army and with much riches.*

14 *And in those times there shall many stand up against the king of the south: also the robbers of thy people shall exalt themselves to establish the vision; but they shall fall.*

15 *So the king of the north shall come, and cast up a mount, and take the most fenced cities: and the arms of the south shall not withstand, neither his chosen people, neither shall there be any strength to withstand.*

16 *But he that cometh against him shall do according to his own will, and none shall stand before him: and he shall stand in the glorious land, which by his hand shall be consumed.*

17 *He shall also set his face to enter with the strength of his whole kingdom, and upright ones with him; thus shall he do: and he shall give him the daughter of women, corrupting her: but she shall not stand on his side, neither be for him.*

18 *After this shall he turn his face unto the isles, and shall take many: but a prince for his own behalf shall cause the reproach offered by him to cease; without his own reproach he shall cause it to turn upon him.*

19 *Then he shall turn his face toward the fort of his own land: but he shall stumble and fall, and not be found.*

20 *Then shall stand up in his estate a raiser of taxes in the glory of the kingdom: but within few days he shall be destroyed, neither in anger, nor in battle.*

21 *And in his estate shall stand up a vile person, to whom they shall not give the honour of the kingdom: but he shall come in peaceably, and obtain the kingdom by flatteries.*

22 *And with the arms of a flood shall they be overflown from before him, and shall be broken; yea, also the prince of the covenant.*

23 *And after the league made with him he shall work deceitfully: for he shall come up, and shall become strong with a small people.*

24 *He shall enter peaceably even upon the fattest places of the province; and he shall do that which his fathers have not done, nor his fathers' fathers; he shall scatter among them the prey, and spoil, and riches: yea, and he shall forecast his devices against the strong holds, even for a time.*

25 *And he shall stir up his power and his courage against the king of the south with a great army; and the king of the south shall be stirred up to battle with a very great and mighty army; but he shall not stand: for they shall forecast devices against him.*

26 *Yea, they that feed of the portion of his meat shall destroy him, and his army shall overflow: and many shall fall down slain.*

27 *And both these kings' hearts shall be to do mischief, and they shall speak lies at one table; but it shall not prosper: for yet the end shall be at the time appointed.*

28 *Then shall he return into his land with great riches; and his heart shall be against the holy covenant; and he shall do exploits, and return to his own land.*

29 *At the time appointed he shall return, and come toward the south; but it shall not be as the former, or as the latter.*

30 *For the ships of Chittim shall come against him: therefore he shall be grieved, and return, and have indignation against the holy covenant: so shall he do; he shall even return, and have intelligence with them that forsake the holy covenant.*

31 *And arms shall stand on his part, and they shall pollute the sanctuary of strength, and shall take away the daily sacrifice, and they shall place the abomination that maketh desolate.*

32 *And such as do wickedly against the covenant shall he corrupt by flatteries: but the people that do know their God shall be strong, and do exploits.*

33 *And they that understand among the people shall instruct many: yet they shall fall by the sword, and by flame, by captivity, and by spoil, many days.*

34 *Now when they shall fall, they shall be helped with a little help: but many shall cleave to them with flatteries.*

35 *And some of them of understanding shall fall, to try them, and to purge, and to make them white, even to*

the time of the end: because it is yet for a time appointed.

> *This beast of a man would also be a precursor of the persecution an end-time global dictator exercises against Israel during the Great Tribulation hour.*

The Wars between the South and the North

From verse 5 we begin to see a powerful struggle taking place between the kings of the South—Egypt—and the kings of the North—Assyria, today's Syria. These nations were constantly at each other's throats, alternating victories. It was a see-saw world of power-grabbing, palace intrigue, and battle fatigue for supreme command of the region. Finally, a scheme was devised to put an end to these constant wars that were taking such a great toll on the people and their respective governments.

This was the plan: Ptolemy II had a daughter, Berenice, and it was decided that if she would marry Antiochus II of Syria a union designed to create a long and lasting peace in the area could be forged. However, even the best laid plans of kings and princesses often do not meet all expectations, and since it was a forced marriage, Antiochus II of Syria hated the arrangement. However, for political reasons, he chose to live with what he disliked. But when the king of Egypt, Ptolemy II, died, Antiochus realized he suddenly had a golden opportunity to get rid of his spouse—which he did. He divorced her and took back his original wife, Laodice.

The ancient soap opera continued to play out when Laodice,

overcome with jealousy, had Berenice poisoned along with most of her family. In the end, the hoped-for peace between Egypt and Assyria did not hold. In fact, this was only the beginning of the shedding of blood between the powers of the north and south. Other high profile names to surface during the next four centuries would be men such as Ptolemy Euergetes, Seleucus Callinicus, Antiochus III, and Ptolemy Philopator, along with the wicked Antiochus Epiphanes who, upon returning from Egypt after having amassed great wealth, began to show his unnatural hatred toward the Jews, an attitude best described by the phrase, "His heart shall be against the holy covenant" (v. 28). This beast of a man would also be a precursor of the persecution an end-time global dictator exercises against Israel during the Great Tribulation hour. We have seen earlier that Antiochus was the designated archetype of the "future man of iniquity"—the Antichrist yet to come. I believe he will soon be on the scene as the clock of history winds down and brings us to the time of the end.

It is impossible to do justice to the history that takes place between verses 1 and 35 without writing a major compendium on the prophecies and their actual fulfillment. There are already many commentaries available that deal with such issues. For our purpose, however, the most important, underlying message of these first thiry-five verses is this:

- They contain 135 Bible prophecies that have been 100 percent fulfilled.
- There is no supportive evidence in history to contradict any of the 135 prophecies, i.e., everything prophesied has come true.
- They provide a convincing introduction to end-time events—a period of time in world history that is rapidly approaching.

• Prophecies still to come in this chapter can be expected to be fulfilled in the same manner as the 135 prophecies were in the first thirty-five verses of Daniel chapter eleven.

With that brief background, we can now proceed to the futuristic nature of Daniel's revelation which begins in verse 36.

36 *And the king shall do according to his will; and he shall exalt himself, and magnify himself above every god, and shall speak marvellous things against the God of gods, and shall prosper till the indignation be accomplished: for that that is determined shall be done.*

37 *Neither shall he regard the God of his fathers, nor the desire of women, nor regard any god: for he shall magnify himself above all.*

38 *But in his estate shall he honour the God of forces: and a god whom his fathers knew not shall he honour with gold, and silver, and with precious stones, and pleasant things.*

39 *Thus shall he do in the most strong holds with a strange god, whom he shall acknowledge and increase with glory: and he shall cause them to rule over many, and shall divide the land for gain.*

40 *And at the time of the end shall the king of the south push at him: and the king of the north shall come against him like a whirlwind, with chariots, and with horsemen, and with many ships; and he shall enter into the countries, and shall overflow and pass over.*

41 *He shall enter also into the glorious land, and many countries shall be overthrown: but these shall escape*

*out of his hand, even Edom, and Moab, and the chief
of the children of Ammon.*

42 *He shall stretch forth his hand also upon the countries: and the land of Egypt shall not escape.*

43 *But he shall have power over the treasures of gold and
of silver, and over all the precious things of Egypt:
and the Libyans and the Ethiopians shall be at his
steps.*

44 *But tidings out of the east and out of the north shall
trouble him: therefore he shall go forth with great
fury to destroy, and utterly to make away many.*

45 *And he shall plant the tabernacles of his palace
between the seas in the glorious holy mountain; yet he
shall come to his end, and none shall help him.*

> *He will be an absolute dic-
> tator who, like a child,
> demands his own way and
> expects to accomplish all his
> objectives on his own terms.*

The King of the Time of the End

Up until this point in chapter eleven, the 135 prophecies that
deal with the Persian and Grecian empires have been fulfilled
with minute precision—every event verified and documented
by the rigors of both religious and secular history, and culmi-
nating with the "end days" of the wicked Antiochus Epiphanes

(164 B.C.). Now, however—beginning with verse 36—we find ourselves in new territory. Here we suddenly confront prophecies that have not yet been fulfilled. Nothing here can be related to previously predicted and fulfilled historical events, which means we are now stepping into areas that speak of a yet-to-be-fulfilled future—specifically the life and times of the Antichrist who will wield his worldwide influence for seven years as he and his worldwide reign lead up to the second coming of our Lord Jesus Christ.

As this Antichrist of the Great Tribulation is described in Daniel's revelation, we learn again that he does as he pleases, magnifies himself above every god, speaks terrible things against God, and prospers until the "indignation" is finished (Revelation 14:10). He will be an absolute dictator who, like a child, demands his own way and expects to accomplish all his objectives on his own terms. The Antichrist will blaspheme the one true God and will do monstrous things against the God of gods. You'll recall that the same thing was said of his predecessor—the little horn of Daniel 7:25. In simple terms, the Antichrist will be a madman who claims he is deity, one who will run the "end-time show" in an attempt to obliterate Israel. The Scripture also adds that he will not "regard the desire of women" (v. 37). Some scholars have suggested this to mean that the Antichrist will not engage in the normal physical desires which a man has for a woman. This idea, however, does not fit the context. More in line is the thought that this is a specific urge or craving the women of Israel had to become the mother of the Messiah, fulfilling Micah 5:2 and Isaiah 9:6–7. Therefore, because the Antichrist hates God—and hates Christ—he has no regard for the Savior, the desire of women for centuries to bear and deliver the Messiah. The Antichrist will hate Jesus so much, and become so violently opposed to everything for which He stands, that he not only refuses to bow down and worship the Savior, but also executes those who do (Revelation 13:15; 20:4).

The Great Deceiver

Some have suggested that the Antichrist will be a Jew who has departed from the God of his fathers, *Yahweh*. However, this cannot be the case because according to prophecy he must emerge from the revived Roman Empire and must therefore be a "son" born within the European Union. It's my belief that we can expect the Antichrist to be a Gentile who defects from his religious upbringing and becomes an avowed believer in, and promoter of, the philosophy of the New Age movement. I encourage you to pay careful attention to this movement in the days ahead as you see its power manifested around you. Remember that New Age thinking is much more harmful than a few innocent crystals, shamans, incense-burning bookstores, Tarot cards, and some mystical, put-you-to-sleep music. Pay particular attention to the words that advocates of the New Age movement use, such as "you are little gods," or "you can be like a god," or "you can make your own happiness," or "you need to do nothing more than center yourself in your own consciousness," along with a constant repetition of the phrase "I am," a not so subtle suggestion that they regard themselves as good as miniature gods. These words and phrases put them on the precipice of blasphemy, and create an apostate atmosphere in which the Antichrist will feel very much at home. We who have ears to hear must remember that God is revealing these final truths to Daniel. Today this book is now open and unsealed. The predicted events are happening and "the time of the end" has arrived.

> *He (the Antichrist) will*
> *heap masses of money and*
> *an abundance of material*
> *things upon the have-nots of*
> *the world.*

Not only is the Antichrist a great opponent of almighty God and His people, but he is also a great deceiver. He comes as a man of peace, making a binding covenant with Israel at the beginning of the seventieth seven of years. This pact will tie Israel so tightly to the Antichrist that Israel will, for all practical purposes, be an "arm" of this revived Roman ruler in the Middle East. Therefore, any attack on Israel will be regarded as an attack on the Antichrist himself.

But when Israel is later attacked by Egypt and Russia (kings of the South and the North) we will begin to see the pact with Israel for the sham it really is. How deceitful will the Antichrist be? Daniel 11:38 says, "He shall honour the God of forces: and a god whom his fathers knew not shall he honour with gold, and silver, and with precious stones, and pleasant things." The Antichrist will get his own way because of his ability to beguile virtually all the nations of earth with his smooth tongue and New Age-like thinking, wresting the entire world under his control. The gods he honors will be New Age gods, people, and personalities, all minor gods of whom he, the Antichrist, is chief. It will be a Robin Hood scenario where he takes from the rich and gives to the poor—an activity for which he will receive uncritical, rave reviews. He will heap masses of money and an abundance of material things upon the have-nots of the world, and they will honor and follow him as so many lemmings over the precipice until he ultimately gets what he wants. But watch out, because at that point this E.U. Pied Piper will rid himself of his most ardent followers.

Revelation 13:1–18 is an important reminder of the global extent of this dictator. For your easy reference, I'm listing the entire passage. It's important that you read this text in its entirety because of its detailed predictions of what this "beast," or Antichrist, will resemble:

And I stood upon the sand of the sea, and saw a beast rise up out of the sea, having seven heads and ten horns, and upon his horns ten crowns, and upon his heads the name of blasphemy. And the beast which I saw was like unto a leopard, and his feet were as the feet of a bear, and his mouth as the mouth of a lion: and the dragon gave him his power, and his seat, and great authority. And I saw one of his heads as it were wounded to death; and his deadly wound was healed: and all the world wondered after the beast. And they worshipped the dragon which gave power unto the beast: and they worshipped the beast, saying, Who is like unto the beast? who is able to make war with him? And there was given unto him a mouth speaking great things and blasphemies; and power was given unto him to continue forty and two months. And he opened his mouth in blasphemy against God, to blaspheme his name, and his taber-nacle, and them that dwell in heaven. And it was given unto him to make war with the saints, and to overcome them: and power was given him over all kindreds, and tongues, and nations. And all that dwell upon the earth shall worship him, whose names are not written in the book of life of the Lamb slain from the foundation of the world. If any man have an ear, let him hear. He that leadeth into captivity shall go into captivity: he that kil-leth with the sword must be killed with the sword. Here is the patience and the faith of the saints. And I beheld another beast coming up out of the earth; and he had two horns like a lamb, and he spake as a dragon. And he exerciseth all the power of the first beast before him, and causeth the earth and them which dwell therein to worship the first beast, whose deadly wound was healed. And he doeth great wonders, so that he maketh fire come down from heaven on the earth in the sight of men, And deceiveth them that dwell on the earth by the means of those miracles which he had power to do in the sight of the beast; saying to them that dwell on the earth, that they should make an image to the beast, which had the wound by a sword, and did live. And he had power to give life unto the image of the beast, that the image of the beast should both speak, and cause that as many as would not worship the image of the beast should be killed. And he causeth all, both small and great, rich and poor, free and bond, to receive a mark in their right hand, or in their foreheads: And that no man might buy or sell, save he that had the mark, or the name of the beast, or the number of his name. Here is wisdom. Let him that hath understanding count the number of the beast: for it is the number of a man; and his number is Six hundred threescore and six.

Here is a "beast" who will be killed and then resurrected as Christ was (Daniel 11:45; Revelation 12:3). To ensure that his power base remains unchallenged, he will insist that the mark 666 be given to all—rich and poor, free or bond. This mark on their foreheads or in their right hands will be mandatory for buying something as simple as a loaf of bread. Unknown to many Christians, these numbers, in various forms, are already being prepared as identification tags on products going in and out of the European Union. Recently, one thousand Greek Orthodox priests and nuns conducted protest marches in Athens against an upcoming I.D. they claim contains the number 666. Things are moving at a quickening pace, but none of what we are presently experiencing could possibly be understood until our time—the "latter days." Until then, Daniel would remain a "sealed book," closed until the time of the end. Only at that appointed time would the book be unsealed and revealed—its mysteries brought to light. That hour has arrived.

> *If one took the name Meshech*
> *back to its origin, it would*
> *be Meshech, then Mosach,*
> *then Moscoti, then Moscovi,*
> *and finally, Moscow.*

The Seventieth Week Is Rapidly Approaching

In verse 40 we read, "And at the time of the end shall the king of the south push at him: and the king of the north shall come against him like a whirlwind, with chariots, and with horsemen, and with many ships; and he shall enter into the countries, and shall overflow and pass over." This king of the South is Egypt, combined with a federation of Arab nations that will unite with Egypt. These countries are listed in Ezekiel 38:5–6 as Persia (modern-day Iran and Iraq), Ethiopia, Lybia, and Togarmah (Turkey). Syria is mentioned in Isaiah 17:1, and the listing continues in Psalm 83:4–8 as Edom, Moab, Ammon (Jordan), Gebal and Tyre (Lebanon), and the Philistines (Palestine). The king of the North, Russia, also appears on the scene, coming from the north as prophesied in Ezekiel 38:15 and 39:2. Similar references to these northern military movements can be found in Jeremiah 1:13, 6:22, 10:22, and Joel 2:20. In fact, if one draws a line from Palestine of old—Israel today—to the north pole, one must go through Russia, and actually intersect the city of Moscow. Furthermore, Gog, Magog, Meshech, and Tubal are all cities identifiable within Russia today. Furthermore, if one took the name Meshech back to its origin, it would be Meshech, then Mosach, then Moscoti, then Moscovi, and finally, Moscow. The prophecies of Daniel's fourth revelation are now on the edge of fulfillment. The message of verse 40 is taking shape. Since God kept His promises 135 times in the first thirty-five verses of Daniel chapter eleven, there can be no argument that He will keep the promises He made in verses 40 to 45.

The Campaign of Armageddon Begins

As I mentioned earlier, Rabbi Shvili in his book *Reckonings of Redemption,* written in 1935, states: "We Jews can know everything about our future just from the Book of Daniel." How true! Other Jewish Rabbinical scholars clarify the depth of teaching discovered in verses 40–45 of the eleventh chapter of Daniel. Quoting the Midrash Tehillim they state: "There will be three different attacks against Jerusalem at the time of the end." The three military advances mentioned by these Jewish scholars will be observed and explained as we move ahead in our discussion of the forty-two-month Armageddon campaign.

When Russia heads south to do battle, she will be a mighty force as she comes against the Antichrist's army with chariots, horsemen, and many ships. This is the first military wave of the three-pronged Armageddon campaign mentioned in Daniel 11:40 when the king of the South (Egypt and her Arab federation) and the king of the North (Russia) begin their pincer movement. Ezekiel 38:16 says, "And thou shalt come up against my people of Israel, as a cloud to cover the land; it shall be in the latter days, and I will bring thee against my land, that the heathen may know me, when I shall be sanctified in thee, O Gog, before their eyes." Once Russia has made her move, the Antichrist will be furious.

He will enter the "glorious land," Israel.

Here is the upcoming scenario. The Antichrist will sit in Jerusalem—in the Jewish temple at the midpoint of the Tribulation hour—the second three and one-half years, calling himself God. Since he knows that he has only a short time to do his global mischief while incarnated by Satan, he spews forth wrath and hatred. When he hears that Russia and the Arab federation are invading the region, he moves at breakneck speed and puts an end to the militaristic activity of Russia, Egypt, and her hoards. The European Union has taken a position in the conflict and the Antichrist has subdued and driven back the first wave of Russian and Arab invaders. At this point Russia has fled to Siberia (Joel 2:20).

Now the second movement of troops is about to move into the Middle East for another invasion of Israel. Daniel 11:44 states: "Tidings out of the east and out of the north shall trouble him: therefore he shall go forth with great fury to destroy." The Antichrist is now on a bloody rampage. He's heard that great oriental armies are moving down into the region to do battle accompanied by the leftover rag-tag army of Russia that had previously been pushed back to Siberia. This frustrates him as he wonders how he'll be able to fend off two hundred million troops who are out to destroy him (Revelation 9:16). He's now overwhelmed and fears he will be unable to maintain enough of a power base to defend himself. During this juncture, the Antichrist is killed by Gog of Russia (Daniel 11:45). But, as we learned earlier, he suddenly comes back to life, duplicating the resurrection of Jesus Christ—something no one in history has ever done (Revelation 13:3). He flaunts this demonic miracle and uses it to again position himself as a god among men, reestablishing himself when he needs it most—when his reputation and strength are on the line. Because of his miraculous resurrection, all the world worships him (Revelation 13:8).

*Israel became a nation in
1948 but has never been at rest
since that memorable day.*

Israel—a Nation Not at Rest

Verse 45 of this chapter says, "And he shall plant the tabernacles of his palace between the seas in the glorious holy mountain; yet he shall come to his end, and none shall help him." The Bible teaches that the Antichrist is going to plant himself between the seas—the Dead Sea and the Mediterranean. The holy mountain, which is Jerusalem, is where he will then live for three and one-half years after his resurrection, usurping the Jewish throne as he sets himself up as god in the Jewish temple. Second Thessalonians 2:4 declares, "Who opposeth and exalteth himself above all that is called God, or that is worshipped; so that he as God sitteth in the temple of God, showing himself that he is God."

This is the midpoint of the Tribulation period. Russia now invades "the land of unwalled villages against them that are at rest" (Ezekiel 38:11). Israel became a nation in 1948 but has never been at rest since that memorable day. No nation on earth longs more for peace than Israel. Daily newspapers and periodicals constantly portray the restlessness and uneasiness Israel experiences. Soon a western leader out of the European Union will arise and "confirm the covenant" of peace for seven years (Daniel 9:27). However, even this final contract made between the Antichrist and Israel will be short-lived, lasting only forty-two months, after which Russia strikes, aligned with Egypt and her confederation of Arabs. This, I repeat, is that first wave of military force marching against Israel in the Armageddon campaign.

Then China and the remnants of Russia's fallen army join in the fray for the second wave of the Armageddon campaign, as two hundred million soldiers move against Israel—not a difficult assignment for a nation which, in the next decade, will boast a population of more than 1.4 billion people. They will march out of the Orient downward across the areas of Iraq and Syria. Revelation 16:12 says, "The sixth angel poured out his vial upon the great river Euphrates; and the water thereof was dried up, that the way of the kings of the east might be prepared." This second wave of gigantic military power eliminates one-third of earth's inhabitants (Revelation 9:18). In spite of this colossal power, China and Russia are also defeated.

Finally, in the third and closing scene of the Armageddon campaign, the Antichrist and his armies battle Christ in what becomes the war to end all wars. Armageddon, or Har-Megeddo, is the gathering place (Revelation 16:16). From there the armies march to the valley of Jehoshaphat (Joel 3:2). Then Zechariah 14:2 occurs as "all nations gather against Jerusalem to battle." The Antichrist has been doing everything in his power during his final forty-two months to pour out venom on his enemies, but now he speaks the ultimate blasphemy by saying, "I will stop the King of Kings from coming to power." Egotistically, he believes he will also be victorious against the Lord of hosts. Revelation 19:19 sets the stage for this apocalyptic event: "I saw the beast, and the kings of the earth, and their armies, gathered together to make war against Christ that sat on the horse, and against his army."

In Revelation 19:11, Christ appears on a white horse to rule as King of Kings and Lord of Lords. But stubborn and rebellious to the end, the Antichrist insists he will never be defeated by any enemy, including Christ. But this time he's wrong because Christ destroys him with the brightness of His coming (2 Thessalonians 2:8). Christ then takes this beast—the global dictator—along with the false prophet who headed up the world church—and casts them both into a lake of fire (Revelation 19:20). A thousand years later, when Satan is thrown into that same lake of fire, the beast and the false prophet are still in existence, suffering the torment of hell forever and forever.

Again, this final reminder: If God proved himself 135 times in the earlier portion of Daniel chapter eleven, He will surely fulfill these remaining prophecies—and not just some day, but in our day. When will these events take place? At the time of the end (Daniel 11:4; 12:4). It's later than you think. Here's why. The ancient Jewish writing—Avodah Zara 3B—states: "The war of Gog and Magog [Russia] will be one of the key events to usher in the Messianic Era." The revered Jerusalem Targum adds: "At the end of days, Gog and Magog shall march against Jerusalem, but perish by the hand of Messiah." Ezekiel 39:6 verifies this. The stage is now set for the Antichrist to appear. Then seven years after the evil one's dominion of the international scene, Jesus Christ returns to rule on earth in majesty and great glory for one thousand years—the explosive finale to this great Book of Daniel, and our focus in chapter twelve.

Final Mysteries Unsealed

WHAT WE HAVE referred to as the "fourth" vision of Daniel that began in chapter ten, now reaches its grand climax in chapter twelve with its prophecies about the Great Tribulation, the resurrection of Old Testament saints, the sealing of prophecy until the time of the end, and the abomination of desolation. Everything we have studied to this point has been prologue to the magnificent conclusion of Daniel's prophecy. We begin chapter twelve with references to Daniel's people—the Jews—and to the archangel Michael, the protector of the nation of Israel—an assignment that has already been a full-time job for him throughout the ages and, in some ways, has only just begun.

DANIEL 12:1–3

1 *And at that time shall Michael stand up, the great prince which standeth for the children of thy people: and there shall be a time of trouble, such as never was since there was a nation even to that same time: and at that time thy people shall be delivered, every one that shall be found written in the book.*

2 *And many of them that sleep in the dust of the earth shall awake, some to everlasting life, and some to shame and everlasting contempt.*

3 *And they that be wise shall shine as the brightness of
the firmament; and they that turn many to righteousness as the stars for ever and ever.*

While Michael has been the protective overseer of the Jews
throughout their history, his work will become even more critical in the days ahead. The end-time reality for the Jews, according to prophecy, will deteriorate into something worse than
anything anyone has ever witnessed in world history.
Therefore, when you and I think we have it difficult at any
given moment, we must remember that the pain and sorrow we
may be suffering will pale into insignificance when compared
with the trials and tribulations yet to come to so many.
Jeremiah 30:7 says, "Alas! for that day is great, so that none is
like it: it is even the time of Jacob's trouble; but he shall be
saved out of it."

Jesus confirmed Jeremiah's prophecy in Matthew 24:21 when
He said, "For then shall be great tribulation, such as was not
since the beginning of the world to this time, no, nor ever shall
be." However, Jesus says that Michael the protector will also be
there on the scene, doing battle with Satan in the heavenlies
(Revelation 12:7–8). In Daniel 12:1 we see Michael "standing
for the people of Israel." Why will Michael be there? So that the
Jews might be saved physically. That's Michael's job, and the
Jews—at the time of the end—will never need his assistance
more than during this time of "Jacob's trouble"—that period
during the Tribulation hour when Russia marches down to the
Middle East after the Antichrist has broken his peace contract
with Israel—forty-two months after the contract has been in
effect. Everything will be relatively smooth sailing up to that
time, the epitome of economic and political sweetness and light,
and then *Bam!* Everything is smashed to pieces at the midpoint
of the Tribulation period (Daniel 9:27) as Russia goes up against

"the land of unwalled villages . . . to them that are at rest, that dwell safely, all of them dwelling without walls, and having neither bars nor gates" (Ezekiel 38:11). This is the beginning of the time of great persecution for the Jews as Satan is cast out of heaven, with his primary assignment to obliterate the Jewish people from the face of the earth (Revelation 12:13). For all these reasons, Michael will be there to stand up for his people, as revealed to Daniel in the first verse of chapter twelve.

Those Who Sleep Will Awake

If you are a Jewish person, I want you to know that your Old Testament teaches the promise of a resurrection, and that there will be life beyond the grave. Unfortunately, many Jews do not know that Daniel 12:2 is in the Bible. This end-time event is something one should look forward to if one has come to recognize that the expected Messiah is the Lord Jesus Christ and has received Him as a personal Savior. If you are a Gentile who loves the Jewish people, it is paramount that you share this text with your Jewish friends and encourage them to understand that there will also be a place for them during these end-time events. Here's the scenario—and it is a critical one for us to understand in some detail. It all begins with the resurrection of the righteous at the time of the Rapture.

We read in John 5:28–29, "Marvel not at this: for the hour is coming, in the which all that are in the graves shall hear his voice, And shall come forth; they that have done good, unto the resurrection of life." That is the Rapture. Then "they that have done evil, unto the resurrection of damnation," that is, when the lost are raised at the conclusion of the thousand years—to stand before Jesus Christ at the Great White Throne judgment (Revelation 20:11–15). Revelation 4:1 says, "After this I looked, and, behold, a door was opened in heaven: and the first voice which I heard was as it were of a trumpet talking with me; which said, Come up hither, and I will show thee things which must be hereafter." At this juncture, we who are believers are gone—caught away to be with Christ. This is confirmed in 1 Thessalonians 4:16 which says, "For the Lord himself shall descend from heaven with a shout, with the voice of the archangel, and with the trump of God: and the dead in Christ shall rise first." Then, we who are alive and remain— those who've lived up to this hour—shall be caught up together with them—the dead—in the clouds to meet the Lord in the air.

These are not my thoughts,
but rather the words of God
taken from holy Scripture.

Not a Pretty Sight

At this point, the horrible Tribulation hour begins to unfold. To those who may disagree with what I'm about to write, I would like to say this: I am only the messenger of what is stated categorically in God's Word. These are not my thoughts, but rather the words of God taken from holy Scripture. So during this time of Tribulation, great numbers of both Jews and Gentiles will be killed for refusing to receive the mark of the beast (Revelation 13:15). Revelation 20:4 adds, "And I saw thrones, and they sat upon them, and judgment was given unto them: and I saw the souls of them that were beheaded for the witness of Jesus, and for the word of God, and which had not worshipped the beast, neither his image, neither had received his mark upon their foreheads, or in their hands; and they lived and reigned with Christ a thousand years." This is the resurrection for those who endured the Great Tribulation hour—

those who were saved through the preaching of the 144,000 converted Jews of Revelation 7:4–8. Because of these faithful servants, millions of people—Jews and Gentiles alike—invite Christ into their lives as Savior and Lord. These are the ones who've come out of the Tribulation and who have washed their robes, making them white in the blood of the Lamb. Millions will physically survive the seven-year Tribulation period and will also be saved spiritually.

In Matthew 25:31–46, Christ returns to judge the nations and to begin His thousand-year reign, allowing those who survived the 2,520-day period to enter the millennium in their natural bodies. At this point, the previously raptured saints return with Christ (Jude 14). That's the moment when He returns as King of Kings and Lord of Lords (Revelation 19:16). The armies of heaven follow Him to the descending Holy City—the new Jerusalem which hovers above the earthly Jerusalem—for one thousand years. This city, containing twelve gates, honors each of the twelve Jewish patriarchs of the Old Testament by inscribing their names on the gates. How do the Jews arrive in this scenario? Simply answered—the resurrection of Jewish believers in this chapter, verse 2. Millions who died during the Tribulation hour, of both Jews and Gentiles, plus all believing Old Testament Jews covering a period of four thousand years, are raised to live with Christ for one thousand years, at this juncture, when our Savior returns as King of Kings and Lord of Lords (Revelation 19:16; 20:4). These Old Testament Jews strongly believed in and looked forward to Messiah's first and second coming and founded their faith in Him as their redeemer—based on Isaiah 53 and Psalm 22.

These resurrected Jews who lived a holy life, such as Daniel, receive rewards just as the Church did at the judgment seat of Christ (2 Corinthians 5:10; Romans 14:10; 2 Timothy 4:7–8; Revelation 4:10–11). So whether we are Jews or Gentile believers, there will be rewards for all the faithful. Remember that all these saints assemble at this time for one reason only: to live and reign with Christ for one thousand years. If you do not believe that Jews and Christians rule equally in Christ's kingdom on earth, I urge you to re-study Ephesians 2:14–22 and Revelation chapters twenty-one and twenty-two, the basis for this glorious promise. All this—although not in such detail—is what Daniel is being told in his vision.

4 *But thou, O Daniel, shut up the words, and seal the book, even to the time of the end: many shall run to and fro, and knowledge shall be increased.*

5 *Then I Daniel looked, and, behold, there stood other two, the one on this side of the bank of the river, and the other on that side of the bank of the river.*

6 *And one said to the man clothed in linen, which was upon the waters of the river, How long shall it be to the end of these wonders?*

7 *And I heard the man clothed in linen, which was upon the waters of the river, when he held up his right hand and his left hand unto heaven, and sware by him that liveth for ever that it shall be for a time, times, and an half; and when he shall have accomplished to scatter the power of the holy people, all these things shall be finished.*

8 *And I heard, but I understood not: then said I, O my Lord, what shall be the end of these things?*

9 *And he said, Go thy way, Daniel: for the words are closed up and sealed till the time of the end.*

10 *Many shall be purified, and made white, and tried; but the wicked shall do wickedly: and none of the wicked shall understand; but the wise shall understand.*

11 *And from the time that the daily sacrifice shall be taken away, and the abomination that maketh desolate set up, there shall be a thousand two hundred and ninety days.*

12 *Blessed is he that waiteth, and cometh to the thousand three hundred and five and thirty days.*

13 *But go thou thy way till the end be: for thou shalt rest, and stand in thy lot at the end of the days.*

Today, we understand how it will all work.

Shut Up the Words . . . Seal Up the Book

Daniel is told in no uncertain terms that his vision is not for today—and that his revelation will only be understood at the time of the end. For this reason many of the prophecies dealing with the revived Roman Empire, mentioned in Daniel chapter two in the form of the image, as well as the four beasts so accurately described in Daniel chapter seven, would not be understood until the time of the end when the book would be unsealed and revealed.

Historically, none of Daniel's vision made much sense to Bible scholars until 1890, when Dr. Gabaelein began to teach that a revived Roman Empire would come into play during the time of the end. Therefore, the terminology "shut up the words until the time of the end" only became operative in an unprecedented way at the beginning of the twentieth century. This is when we also began to understand clearly that a great nation would march against Israel (Ezekiel 38 and 39) and that this enemy would come from the north. We've already seen in Daniel 11:40 how the king of the South (Egypt) and the king of the North (Russia) would unite to engage in a blitzkrieg, the likes of which the world has never seen previously. No one could make much sense of Daniel's vision until certain world events began to reveal themselves to God's servants.

Today, we understand how it will all happen. But when does it occur? "When many run to and fro and knowledge is increased." There is a dual interpretation in this text. First, travel is reaching unparalleled proportions and knowledge is doubling every twenty-two months. The secondary meaning is that during the time of the end an inordinate fascination for knowledge about latter-day predictions would increase, with people running "to and fro" to learn everything possible concerning the prophecies about the returning King. This is where we are today in this sequence of end-time events. Soon, the Savior will call His Church away to be with Him, after which He returns seven years later, with His people, to rule and reign. It's all beginning to take shape—just as the Holy Spirit, through Daniel, said it would.

Time, Times, and a Half Time

Again, Daniel is joined by two angels who come to give him further insight into historical matters concerning the time of the end. Daniel remains inquisitive. He wants to know what is going to take place in the long run—and he is especially curious as to what will happen to his people, the Jews, during the latter days before the Messiah appears. The one angel responds by saying that time, times, and a half time will bring all these things to a conclusion. What things, and what is meant by this expression? The angel is referring to the terrible battle that takes place in Daniel chapter eleven when the king of the South (Egypt) ultimately invades Israel, leading an Arab federation and joined by the king of the North (Russia). This first wave of troops was discussed in chapter eleven. Next, China enters the fray with her two hundred million soldiers, accompanied by the remnants of Russia's previously defeated army, for the second wave of the Armageddon campaign (Daniel 11:44). This is the information Daniel received, but it was not necessarily the message he wanted to hear.

But what about the seemingly cryptic phrase that time, times, and a half time will bring all these things to a conclusion? Remember that Russia begins her move into the area during the middle of the Tribulation hour—just after the Antichrist breaks his peace treaty with Israel. Time=one year; times=two more years; and a half time=half a year, the total of which is three and one-half years—precisely the concluding portion of the Tribulation period. The forty-two months of Revelation 13:5 are translated as 1,260 days in Revelation 11:3 and 12:6. These terrible battles will occur for forty-two months, right up to the exact moment that the beast and his armies battle Jesus Christ as recorded in Revelation 19:11–21. This is the third and final portion of the Armageddon campaign as thoroughly explained in the previous chapter. Then as Christ appears, the words of Isaiah 2:4 become a reality: "He shall judge among the nations, and shall rebuke many people: and they shall beat their swords into plowshares, and their spears into pruninghooks: nation shall not lift up sword against nation, neither shall they learn war any more." But it is going to take the real Prince—the Lord Jesus Christ—to bring history to this final, tranquil conclusion, the one whose name is the "Prince of Peace" (Isaiah 9:6).

The apostle Paul said that tribulation works patience within us. It makes us into something.

Tribulation Works Patience

At this time, because of the mayhem and terror that's taking place in the Holy Land, the people will flee and be scattered. Matthew 24:16–21 says, "Then let them which be in Judaea flee into the mountains: Let him which is on the housetop not come down to take any thing out of his house: Neither let him which is in the field return back to take his clothes. And woe unto them that are with child, and to them that give suck in those days! But pray ye that your flight be not in the winter, neither on the sabbath day: For then shall be great tribulation, such as was not since the beginning of the world to this time, no, nor ever shall be."

Imagine how Daniel must have felt as he once again heard the prophecies of gloom and doom coming from the mouths of two angels who informed him that everything he now heard was for the time of the end.

The angel said one more thing. It was about many being purified, or made white, people who would have understanding and also about those who were wicked, and who, in their wickedness, would not be able to understand the things of God. First Corinthians 2:14 says that the natural man, the one who is unsaved, does not understand the things of God. To such people they are foolishness. They can't understand them because they have no spiritual discernment. On the other hand,

God's people—especially those who've gone through the mill—will have divine insight into these things because they, as God's faithful servants, have experienced such trials and have been purified through these times of testing.

The apostle Paul said that tribulation works patience within us. It makes us into something. Therefore, those who have been through pain and suffering—but who, in the process, have remained close to the Lord, and have read His Word, and have prayed in faith, believing, and have understood the things of God through the Holy Spirit's enlightenment—will have all these predictions revealed to them. But those who have hardened their hearts through wickedness will go to the time of the end totally ignorant of and carelessly indifferent to the latter-day predictions.

1,260 days . . . 1,290 days

If you've done the arithmetic found in this text, you may be wondering how the angels come up with 1,260, then 1,290, and then 1,335 days. Again, the Word of God is always meticulously correct and on schedule. With this in mind, an announcement is made that soon the millennial Kingdom will be established, but that a time of consecration is first necessary. To help us understand why this is so necessary, let's take a quick side-trip to 2 Chronicles 30:2–4 where we read, "The king had taken counsel, and his princes, and all the congregation in Jerusalem, to keep the passover in the second month. For they could not keep it at that time, because the priests had not sanctified themselves sufficiently, neither had the people gathered themselves together to Jerusalem. And the thing pleased the king and all the congregation." King Hezekiah said that there could be no Passover because there was a need to consecrate the priests—something that would take thirty days. This is a beautiful picture of why an additional thirty-day period will be necessary for

God's people to prepare themselves spiritually to rule and reign with Christ for the greatest event in history.

So, as we look at the additional number, 1,290 days, instead of seeing a discrepancy, we simply need to investigate other portions of Scripture, as we just did, to see the reason. But there's another forty-five-day period mentioned in our text. Here's why: When Christ returns, He judges the nations and their people, and His decree decides whether or not they're qualified to enter His glorious kingdom for a thousand years (Matthew 25:31–46). This judgment undoubtedly takes an additional forty-five days! Thus, we end up with a total of seventy-five days in addition to the 1,260 days. There is no contradiction. Here's why—forty-five days are needed to determine who enters the millennial period, and thirty days are needed to train God's people for Kingdom service for administering the laws of the Kingdom, as described in Matthew chapters five through seven.

Now as we come to the final verse of the Book of Daniel, this great saint and man of God is in his nineties. The angel tells him to "go his way till the end be: for he shall rest, and stand in his lot at the end of his days." The angel is simply saying that there will be a soon-approaching moment when Daniel will die and rest from his labors. But the angel adds that a glorious day is coming when Daniel and all believing Jews shall stand up and be raised from the dead to rule and reign with Christ. One group of saints, who lived through the Tribulation period, are selected in Matthew 25:31–45 and enter the Kingdom in their natural bodies. Then there's the group of believers who died during the Tribulation hour and are resurrected at approximately the time the Jewish Old Testament saints are raised. These resurrected Old Testament saints and Tribulation believers will dwell in the Holy City in glorified bodies and will, together, rule and reign with Jesus Christ for a thousand years along with the raptured believers who return with the Lord.

That's why the names of the twelve Jewish patriarchs and the twelve apostles are mentioned upon the gates and the foundations of the Holy City. They represent all resurrected believers from among both Jews and Christians. May I reiterate what I've just stated so that no one can misinterpret or misunderstand the portion of Scripture just analyzed. There will be four groups sharing Christ's kingdom for one thousand years.

1. The believers who were raptured and who return with Christ seven years later in their glorified bodies (Jude 14; Revelation 19:14).

2. The believers who are selected at Christ's return and are invited to enter the kingdom in their physical bodies (Matthew 25:34).

3. The Old Testament Jewish believers covering a period of four thousand years who are raised from the dead at Christ's return to enter the kingdom in glorified bodies similar to the raptured of group one (Daniel 12:2).

4. The believers, both Jews and Gentiles, who died for Christ during the Tribulation period and are raised from the dead upon the Savior's second coming (Revelation 20:4).

At this point, the angel is saying to Daniel: "Hallelujah! You will be there among them! You've been through tough times, Daniel, and have been faithful to the end. Daniel, you will be greatly rewarded."

Personally, I believe that Daniel will be one of the rulers during that thousand-year reign of Christ on earth. Daniel certainly had great administrative experience serving under six kings.

However, the greatest moment for this man who prayed fearlessly in front of an open window, who slept serenely one night in a den of some two hundred lions, who was lied about and set up to be killed by his palace "friends," will be the moment when he serves the King of Kings, the Lord Jesus Christ, for a thousand years—a time when you and I shall also share in God's blessings.

And thus we come to the close of the Book of Daniel, and a look at the final end-time mysteries that have now been unsealed. We have seen how the Book of Daniel clearly demonstrates the sovereign rule of almighty God over the affairs of men. We have seen prophecy after prophecy fulfilled, all verifiable and documented by secular and religious history. We have observed that God remains in control and will until the time of the end, giving the Gentile world dominance until Christ returns.

> *The Book of Daniel has finally been unsealed and revealed for those who have eyes to see. The time for Christ's return is near.*

He Is Coming Soon

If you are a follower of this One who is coming soon, you can be assured that you will not have to endure the pain and suffering of the Great Tribulation hour. Such cannot be said for those who continue to turn their backs on God, and who choose to live out their own agendas. Now is the time of salvation. Our Lord Jesus Christ is coming soon. Will you be caught up to meet Christ—to later return with Him as he establishes His millennial Kingdom? There are simply too many signs pointing to the time of the end not to take this message to heart. The Book of Daniel has finally been unsealed and revealed for those who have eyes to see. The time for Christ's return is near.

It is my prayer that you have not read this book just as so much interesting ancient history. It is much more than that. It is a carefully crafted blueprint for the time of the end. But the key to understanding this book is not in being able to understand every nuance, each beast, the little horn, or any other veiled prophecy contained in this work. Instead, it is in knowing the living Word—the Lord Jesus Christ—the One who is coming soon.

I close this volume with a quote from one of the most respected biblical scholars of our era, Dr. John F. Walvoord, who stated in his book *Daniel: The Key to Prophetic Revelation:*

> For Christians living in the age of grace and searching for understanding of these difficult days which may be bringing to a close God's purpose in His church, the book of Daniel, as never before, casts a broad light upon contemporary events foreshadowing the consummation which may not be far distant. If God is reviving His people Israel politically, allowing the church to drift into indifference and apostasy, and permitting the nations to move toward centralization of political power, it may not be long before the time of the end will overtake the world. Many who look for the coming of the Lord anticipate their removal from the earth's scene before the final days of the time of the Gentiles are fulfilled.

When the plan of God has run its full course, it will be evident then with even more clarity than at present that God has not allowed a word to fall to the ground. As Christ said while on earth, "Till heaven and earth pass, one jot or one tittle shall in no wise pass from the law, till all be fulfilled" (Matthew 5:18).[1]

To which I only add, Come quickly, Lord Jesus. Maranatha!

[1] John F. Walvoord, *Daniel: The Key to Prophetic Revelation* (Chicago: Moody Press, 1971), 297.

About the Author

Dr. Jack Van Impe has preached the gospel face-to-face to more than any evangelist except Dr. Billy Graham. More than one million souls have been saved through Jack Van Impe Ministries. He and his wife, Rexella, have delivered the gospel message to audiences totaling ten million in citywide crusades across America and Canada. Today, the couple co-anchors *Jack Van Impe Presents,* a news-style television and radio program examining current headlines in the light of Bible prophecy. *Jack Van Impe Presents* is carried in twenty-five thousand cities in North America, and reaches 160 nations around the globe.

The Van Impes have received nineteen Angel Awards for excellence in media presentation. Dr. Van Impe has written twenty-five books and produced almost one hundred hours of audio and videocassettes with a combined distribution of five million copies. As a leading Christian apologist and promoter of unity within the Body of Christ, Dr. Van Impe has appeared on two hundred talk shows and has been featured in articles in *U. S. News & World Report, Time,* and *Newsweek,* as well as in scores of newspapers. He has been honored by fourteen leading colleges and seminaries with doctoral degrees in the field of theology, and has committed over fourteen thousand verses of Scripture to memory.